SECRETS of the PALM

SECRETS
of the PALM

by Darlene Hansen

International Standard Book Number 0-917086-52-X

Cover artwork by Larry Ortiz
Illustrations by Robin Secher

Printed in the United States of America

Published by ACS Publications, Inc.
P.O. Box 16430
San Diego, CA 92116-0430

First Printing, March 1985
Second Printing, October 1985

DEDICATION

*This book is dedicated to Michael O'Donnell,
an old soul friend.*

Also by ACS Publications, Inc.

PUBLISHER'S NOTE

Since this book deals with health in some areas, caution and common sense should be utilized as the author in no way diagnoses or makes medical judgments. See your preferred health professional for such medical decisions.

CONTENTS

Dedication v

Preface xiii

Introduction xiv

Chapter One   **THE BACK OF THE HAND** .1
        Major and Minor Hands 1
        Texture of the Skin 2
        Hair 2
        Fingernails 3
        Width 5
        Length 5
        Security vs. Insecurity 6
        Test Yourself #1 9

Chapter Two   **HEALTH AND DISEASE AS SHOWN IN THE**
        FINGERNAILS 11
        Color 12
        Shape 13
        Markings 13
        Test Yourself #2 15

Chapter Three   **THE PALM PROPER** 17
        Length of the Palm and Fingers 17
        Arch of the Fingers 19
        Smooth or Knotty 19
        Match Them Up #3 21

Chapter Four   **FINGERPRINT PATTERNS** .22
        Test Yourself #4 26

Chapter Five   **THE THUMB AND FINGERS** 28
        The Thumb 28
        The Fingers 33
        The Phalanges 35
        Test Yourself #5 38

Chapter Six   **THE SHAPE OF THE PALM** 40

The Square Palm 40

The Round Palm 42

The Philosophical Hand 42

The Psychic Hand 42

Diseases Which Can Show in the Palm 45

Combination Hands 48

Combinations 50

Test Yourself #6 54

Chapter Seven   **MOUNTS, DISPLACEMENTS AND MARKINGS** ... 55

The Jupiter Mount 57

The Saturn Mount 58

The Uranus Mount 60

The Mercury Mount 64

The Upper Mars Mount 66

The Luna Mount 66

The Pluto Mount 68

The Neptune Mount 70

The Venus Mount 70

The Sun Mount 73

The Lower Mars Mount 73

Test Yourself #7 75

Chapter Eight   **THE MAJOR LINES IN THE HAND** 78

The Life Line 78

Test Yourself #8.a 85

The Head Line 87

Test Yourself #8.b 90

The Heart Line 92

Match Them Up #8.c 97

Chapter Nine   **THE MINOR LINES OF THE HAND** 98

The Fate Line 98

Test Yourself #9.a 101

The Sun Line 103

The Mercury Line 103

Test Yourself #9.b 105

Union Lines 107

Test Yourself #9.c 110

The Children Lines 110

Match Them Up #9.d 113

The Girdle of Venus 113

Test Yourself #9.e 116

Chapter Ten   **COMPATIBILITY** 117

                       Couple A 118

                       Couple B..................................121

                       Couple C 124

Chapter Eleven **THE WALINSKI FAMILY** 128

Chapter Twelve **EPILOGUE** 171

Bibliography 172

PREFACE

This book is written for and dedicated also to helping both the beginning student in palmistry and the advanced student who is looking for new information. I invite both your questions and responses.

In this book I will use the pronoun "she" as well as the generic "he" so that women are more clearly included. Since his/her or himself/herself are awkward constructions for the readers, these pronouns will be alternated according to chapters. Thus, one chapter will contain all "him's; another all "her's. These pronouns are used in a universal way and are not intended to represent a specific sex.

Received under automatic writing*:

The palm sets the background, the fingers set the mood and the lines set the action. The directions of the lines set the possibilities. They all work together.

---

* Automatic writing is: "writing performed without conscious intention and sometimes without awareness as if of telepathic or spiritual origin." *Encyclopaedia Britannica, Inc.*, William Benton, Publisher, New York, 1966

INTRODUCTION

Did you know that we have information on palmistry as old as 2000 BC? That Aristotle, Alexander the Great, Paracelsus, Honoré de Balzac, Napoleon III and many other important people believed and studied hand reading? And did you know that your tax dollars are going to the study of palm reading? It's true. The Department of Health & Human Services has allotted money to investigate 100,000 prints of palms and fingerprint patterns to see if there is any direct correlation between certain neurological diseases and the finger and palm prints.

The word **chirology**, or hand interpretation, is derived from the Latin word *chir* or *chiro*, meaning "hand," and is a combination of the study of the form of the hand, known as **chirognomy**, and the study of the lines of the hand, known as **chiromancy**. In ancient Greece the people who were responsible for healing with their hands were known as *cheirourgus*, or hand workers. This is where our English word for "surgeon" comes from.[1]

When or where palmistry actually began is unknown, but we do know that it was practiced by the Brahmins of India and that it was known to Aristotle, who supposedly discovered a treatise on the subject written in gold letters. He presented it to his student, Alexander the Great, but it has unfortunately been lost or destroyed.

There are remnants of the ancient study of palmistry throughout history. In a Neolithic burial passage on an island off Brittany there are fingerprint pattern designs that have lasted through time.

In the Old Testament of the Bible there are numerous references to the study of hand reading. For example:

---

1. Benham, William. *The Laws of Scientific Hand Reading*, New York, London: G.P. Putnam's Sons, 1900.

And he said, Wherefore doth my lord thus pursue after his servant? What have I done? Or what evil is in mine hand?

(I Samuel 26:18)

Length of days is in her right hand; and in her left hand riches and honors.

(Proverbs 3:16)

There are a number of Ancient works on palmistry by such noted persons as Anaxagoras, the Greek philosopher, Hippocrates, the Greek physician and the father of medicine, and Galen of Pergamum, the Roman physician of the second century AD. There is also an aboriginal Indian carving several hundred years old in Nova Scotia showing the lines of the palm and fingerprint patterns.

More nerves run from the brain to the area of the palms and fingertips than to any other area of our body. Psychogalvanic responses register here showing stress and anxiety and are one of the reasons this area is useful in lie detector tests. Hence, it should come as no surprise to anyone that health and disease can be seen in the palm and the fingers.

The palm is an indicator of many facets of our being. All we need to do is to clue into the systematic workings of our hands to help us glean more knowledge about ourselves and about others.

I would like to take you on a journey of the map of your hand. This journey will include the fundamentals of palmistry: the back of the hand, the nails, the mounts, and the major and minor lines. This journey will also include the medical research being done on the palm, new information on the misunderstood Girdle of Venus and a chapter on compatibility.

I hope you enjoy your travels!

CHAPTER ONE

THE BACK OF THE HAND

There is nothing in the three worlds for knowledge besides the hand which is given to mankind like a book to read.

— Hastha Sanjeevan

The Major and Minor Hands

The hand a person actively uses is considered the major, or conscious, hand. This shows the way the person is living right now and what talents and attributes she is making use of.

The unconscious, or minor, hand shows the inherited qualities and the possibilities for the future.

Statistically, 92%[2] of people use their right hand for activities. You will come across people who are ambidextrous. In this case, you will initially have to read both hands until you find the major one.

One of the reasons that we may have such a high statistic of right-handed people is social pressure. Many of the objects we use in everyday life, such as scissors, are constructed for the right-handed person. Many left-handed people have been urged to learn how to use their right hands to compensate for this trend.

I have even come across subjects who were forced by their parents to use their right hand because of the old superstition about the left hand being the work of the devil.

In these cases the person's conscious hand is still the left hand,

2. Steinbach, Marten. *Medical Palmistry*, 88. New York: New American Library, 1975.

not the right. Please remember that communication with your client is extremely important so that you can do the best reading possible for that individual.

The Texture of the Skin

The texture of the skin will be an indicator of the emotional sensitivities of the person and will show a propensity to certain occupations.

The softer the skin, the softer the person. The person with baby-fine skin is usually sensitive to others and what they think and feel. She tends to be gentle and experience life deeply. These people will shun outdoor work and activities if possible. You will find them most often in front of a cozy fire reading a good book, at the theater, or at the ballet.

The person with coarser skin needs to be outdoors in order to release physical energies. This person does not care so much what others think. She can live without them. If the skin is also dry to the touch, you know that your client is sensual.

The medium fine skin is the most practical. Here we have a balance of sensitivity and of objectivity.

One question I am often asked when discussing the texture of the hand is, how do I know that the texture of the hand leads to the person's choice of occupations and not vice versa? All I can say to that is, what came first, the chicken or the egg? Why shouldn't people choose their occupation or environment due to their own physiological makeup and sensitivities? After all, the hand of a newborn possesses all the major lines and already shows the psychological makeup of that individual.

Hair

The traditional teaching about body hair was that it symbolized the physical gross form and shows the prevalence of the baser sexual forces in humankind.

That doesn't sound too promising for anyone born of Latin stock who usually does have more body hair than the Orientals or Eastern Indians.

What I have found is that the more hair people have on their bodies, the more physically aggressive those people are. The less hair people have on their bodies, the more they tend to be diplomatic when dealing with others — the velvet glove treatment.

Fingernails

The fingernails, like the palm, have a distinct shape to them and will help disclose the temperament of your client.

There are five basic classifications of the fingernails: the pointed, the conic, the square, the spatulate and the filbert.

The Pointed Nail
This nail (fig. 1.1) is sometimes considered an exaggerated form of the conic nail. The pointed nail is usually found on the psychic or conic palm. It shows nervousness, artistic ability, an idealist, a dreamer or a psychic. Depending on the other markings in the palm, the person with this nail shape might find it very difficult to understand the world. She may be too much of a dreamer and a lover of beauty for the sake of beauty. Hopefully there will be a strong Saturn line with a good thumb and index finger to counterbalance the traits indicated by this nail. Otherwise, the individual might retreat too much from the physical world. Sensitivity is marked.

The Conic Nail
The conic nail (fig. 1.2) is found most often on the conic hand, but can also be found on the square hand. This shape shows a warm, friendly person who enjoys the company of others. It also usually indicates artistic energy.

The Square Nail
This nail (fig. 1.3) is most always found on the square hand. It shows good rational thinking, aggressiveness and a need for order in the person's environment. The thinking tends to be linear, with excellent organizational skills.

The Spatulate Nail
This nail (fig. 1.4) is found on the spatulate or philosophical hand. It is the nail of the critic, the skeptic, the person who is always asking questions. This person has a lot of energy that needs to be released. The individual may be difficult to keep up with, or may scatter her forces through multiple interests and pursuits. The mind is inquiring.

The Filbert Nail
The filbert nail (fig. 1.5) is an exaggeration of the spatulate nail and shows an overabundance of curiosity and emotion. These people are extremely hyper. They often need to learn to slow down and rest from

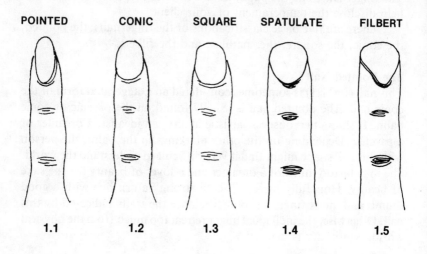

POINTED   CONIC   SQUARE   SPATULATE   FILBERT

1.1   1.2   1.3   1.4   1.5

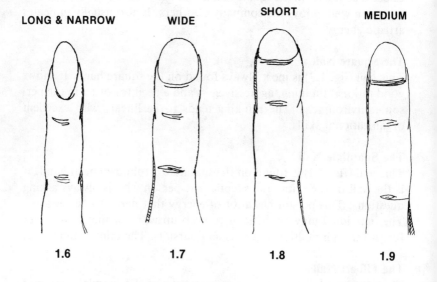

LONG & NARROW   WIDE   SHORT   MEDIUM

1.6   1.7   1.8   1.9

time to time or they may burn themselves out or fall into being a dilettante. Capable of tremendous warmth, they can be very loving, but tend toward intense, short bursts of concentration and enthusiasm.

Width

The width of the nail will indicate the physical energy available to your client.

The Narrow Nail
This nail (fig. 1.6) usually shows a quiet person, one who dislikes arguments because they tax the system. These people tend to have more mental/emotional energy than physical energy.

The Wide Nail
This nail (fig. 1.7) shows an active individual who finds it difficult to sit down. This person has a lot of physical energy and vitality.

Length

The length of the nail acts as a guide to the temperament.

Long Nails
This nail (fig. 1.6) show a gentle person who loves balance and harmony. This is the nail of the perfectionist. The person's need for balance can cause restriction to herself and to others. Everything has to be just so, just right. This person needs to learn that nothing is perfect.

Short Nails
These nails (fig. 1.8) belong to the critic, the complainer, and the aggressive, blunt, outgoing human being. These people have a lot of drive, persistency and inner strength.

Medium Nails
These nails (fig. 1.9) indicate someone right in midstream between the lover of balance and harmony versus the outspoken, persistent person.

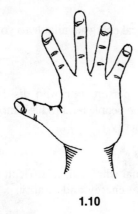

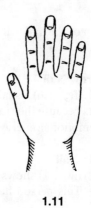

1.10   **1.11**

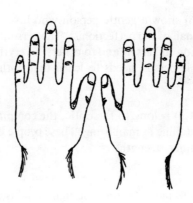

1.12

Security vs. Insecurity

Freedom has a thousand charms to show, that slaves, howe'er contented, never know.

— William Cowper

The space between the hands and between the fingers when laid down on the table will indicate the amount of security or insecurity your client has. The more space, the more freedom. The less space, the more restriction.

The conscious hand will always be compared to the unconscious hand to compare the differences between the present (the major hand) and the past (the minor hand) so this is an immediate register of freedom or confinement. The spacing will change as circumstances change for your client and as your client changes her attitudes about life.

The person with wide spaces between the fingers (fig. 1.10) will show a secure, unconventional nature. She will not be afraid to try new things because she will not be afraid of failure. She will look upon each new experience as an adventure. Such people will be a lot of fun to be with, but on the other side of the coin, they might sometimes prove to be too rash for their own good, getting themselves into hot water.

The narrow space (fig. 1.11) shows a need for security and, in order to maintain that security, the person will be more apt to give in to the conventional mores of the world. She will walk the line rather than rock the boat.

Between the Hands
A large spatial difference between the two hands when they are placed down on a table will show you a person of action. This person is a doer, inclined towards spontaneity.

The closer together the hands, the more the person will think before she acts (fig.1.12).

Hands which are symmetrically aligned show unusual diplomacy and tact, but if the hands touch each other, the person needs someone else to lean on.

Between the Fingers
The space between the Mercury (little) and the Uranus (third) fingers shows the person's independence. The more space, the more independence. A narrow space tends to show a dependent personality (fig. 1.13).

The space between the Uranus and the Saturn (second) fingers

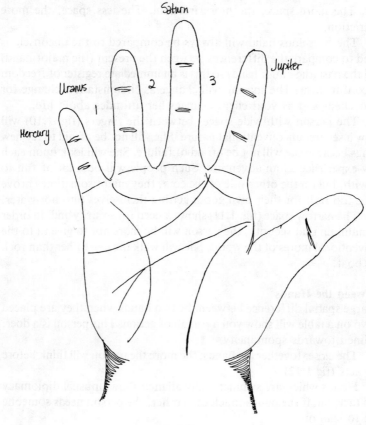

1.13

shows financial security. The more space, the more financially secure the person is. A narrow space shows a restriction on the flow of resources. The person may be putting money away for a rainy day. The space between the Saturn and the Jupiter (index) fingers shows how innovative your client is. The wider the space, the more inventive the person is. A narrow space shows someone who is not into change or variation in their life, especially if the space between the Mercury and the Uranus fingers is also narrow. If, on the other hand, the space between the Mercury and Uranus fingers is wide and the space between the Saturn and Jupiter fingers is narrow, the person likes to be independent, but she does not always follow through with her independent thinking.

Test Yourself #1

1. Explain the difference between the major and the minor hands.
_____
_____
_____

2. Who would be more sensitive to what others think about them — the person with fine skin or coarse skin?
_____

3. Body hair suggests what about your client?
_____

4. Name the five basic classifications of fingernails.
A) _____
B) _____
C) _____
D) _____
E) _____

5. What does the filbert nail tell you and what nail shape is it an exaggeration of?
A) _____
B) _____

6. Which nail speaks of warmth and creative energy?
_____

Which nail shows the dreamer and the lover of beauty?
_____

Which nail shows the critic?
_____

Which nail shows the lover of order?
_____

7. The width of the nail will tell you what about your client?
   _____

8. What one word helps to explain the short nail person?
   _____

9. What one word helps to explain the long nail person?
   _____

10. What does space between the hands and fingers indicate?
    _____

11. What does the space between the following fingers represent?
    Mercury and Uranus _____
    Uranus and Saturn _____
    Saturn and Jupiter _____

12. Symmetrically aligned hands imply what about the person?
    _____

CHAPTER TWO

HEALTH AND DISEASE AS SHOWN IN THE FINGERNAILS

More and more scientists are using the fingernails, hands and finger-prints for diagnosing diseases. The medical profession is not exactly backing the art of palmistry, but many doctors are accepting the facts that the physical body cannot be divorced from the mental and emotional body and that ailments in our physical form can be an indicator of disharmony in the mental and emotional areas.

To make use of this involvement, some universities are offering courses that use the vibratory energy from the hands to heal and soothe physical, emotional and mental problems. At California State University in Long Beach the nursing extension department is offering a course entitled, "Laying on of Hands." John F. Kennedy University, near San Francisco, is offering courses in "Therapeutic Touch" and "Applied Kinesiology or Touch for Health." The concepts behind these courses are the same. They deal with channeled energy and the ability for that energy to heal or to put the body back into balance, which is health. For the majority of us, this would mean that we do not have to rely on artificial means of healing such as pills or shots, but can rely on our own energy source which is definitely healthier and less expensive.

I received the following script through automatic writing on the experience of health:

I would like to talk to you about pain — the opposite of suffering, the component of joy, just conceived incorrectly. No such thing as pain exists, you understand, but sometimes the physical body is so numb it needs the intensity of pleasure you call pain to get through the block of the mental and physical body.

Radiance, health and youth are the natural components of the body — natural, normal and unaccepted because suffering is not involved and most people are into suffering.

Pain is the intensity of joy. Joy is a sin to most human beings, so pain becomes a substitute and accepted behavioral pattern when joy would do very nicely.

Let us first look at some of the physical disorders that can be seen in the fingernails. Let me stress that when I speak of the physical disorders, I am not excluding the emotional, mental or spiritual diseases. These composite bodies manifest themselves in our material form, our physical being, and we have to look at them from this aspect. However, remember no one sign is a positive diagnosis.

Good health is best maintained by balance on all levels: physical, emotional, mental and spiritual. This book is not intended, in any way, to replace competent medical advice. Please seek the appropriate health practitioner to deal with physical problems. However, consider being open to treatment on the emotional and spiritual levels as well. Resolving certain emotional issues can often aid physical recovery. Prayer, meditation and other spiritual pursuits can assist any cure. Facing any problem on a number of levels maximizes the likelihood of a positive, lasting result.

Color

Pink-colored nails generally show health, warmth and the ability to relax and let things be.

Red-colored nails can indicate too much of a good thing. These people often have a lot of energy, and if they do not know how to channel this excess energy, they can become irritable and might do things in a hasty way. Pale fingernails usually show a person who is not outgoing. This can also be the result of anemia, especially if the palm is pale in color as well. Remember, you must always compare the color of the palm and the fingernails with the natural coloring of the person. The pale nail can indicate a lack of good circulation.

Blue fingernails show a definite circulatory problem. These people would benefit from some type of exercise program. Since they might have cardiac problems, the exercise should be recommended by their physicians.

Shape

Narrow, long nails (fig. 2.1) can show delicacy of the lungs and possible problems with allergies or asthma. It is as though the restriction of the width of the nail is a shadowing of the restriction of the respiratory system. According to Cheiro's *Language of the Hand*, nails that are long and narrow can also show consumptive tendencies, but Cheiro was writing in the late nineteenth century when consumption was rampant.

A sensitivity around breathing is often related to hesitation around speech. People may fear to say the "wrong" thing or hurt other people's feelings. Some people with asthma have discovered that speaking their minds can prevent an oncoming asthma attack. Perfectionism and trying to do too many things can also be related to breathing difficulties. Allowing one's self and others to be human helps.

Watchglass nails (fig. 2.2) may indicate problems with the heart, liver or respiratory system. The respiratory problems show up more on the nail which is long and curved, while the heart problem seems to show up more on the nail that is short and curved. Remember, no one sign such as this is enough by itself to assume problems; there will always be more than one sign in the hand pointing to physical sensitivities.

Scooped nails (fig. 2.3) can show nutritional deficiencies and skin disorders. We are what we eat to a large extent. Diet is a very individual matter; there are few truisms that will work for everyone. Listening to your own body and watching its cues can be very helpful in determining which foods really are best for you.

Markings

Ridges that run the width of the nail (fig. 2.4) are known as **Beau's lines** and show acute infection, shock to the system, or the flu. I have seen this line on people who have changed jobs, locations or gone through a divorce. This physical sign reflects psychological as well as physical stress. One's emotional reaction is mirrored in the nail. The growing period of the nail is approximately six months, so a palmist can tell when the client has suffered from the illness or gone through some kind of trauma. During World War I, doctors used this timing method to determine when a soldier had been injured.

Ridges that travel the length of the nail (fig. 2.5) usually show nutritional problems and a predisposition to rheumatism and colitis. Proper diet and regular exercise are exceedingly helpful. Also, an ability

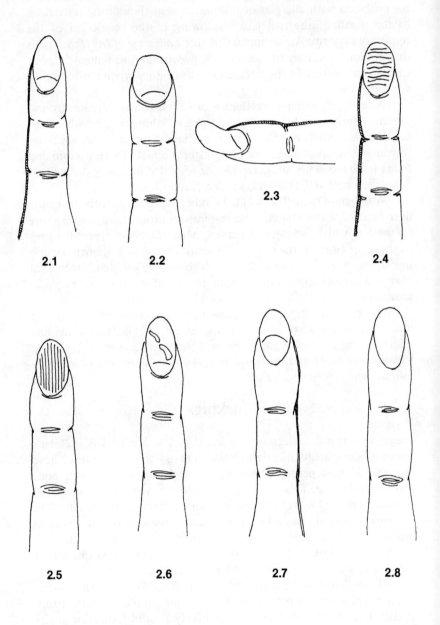

2.1

2.2

2.3

2.4

2.5

2.6

2.7

2.8

to relax can work wonders. Both rheumatism and colitis can be related to an obsessive-compulsive tendency to nitpick, focus on tiny details, be overly concerned with order and predictability. Flowing with life, releasing one's sense of responsibility and need to "do" something can help considerably.

White lines on the fingernail (fig. 2.6), known as **Mee's lines**, can show a heart problem, high fevers and also nervous exhaustion. In the case of nervous exhaustion, the Mee's lines will disappear when the client has had rest.

Often, the issue is not how much the person does, but how the person **feels** about what he does. Some people accomplish a tremendous amount, enjoying every minute of it. Other people do "less" objectively, but feel a sense of pressure, of being burdened. It is the psychological sense of pressure, the stress on the system, which has the biggest impact. Reasonable expectations, faith in the ultimate goodness of life and the ability to relax can all help lessen tension and stress.

The healthy finger will have moons at the quick. When the moons are large and the nail is narrow and shiny, the person might have an overactive thyroid (fig. 2.7).

When no moons are apparent and the nail is thin and brittle, the person might have an underactive thyroid (fig. 2.8). Most doctors check the nails during a routine examination for many of the above clues to health. **Remember, no one sign is a positive diagnosis.**

I do believe, like an unknown writer, that "we do not discover our destiny, we **create** it." Please understand that we are in control of our bodies and many physical problems can be changed by our mental, emotional and/or spiritual attitudes.

Test Yourself #2

1. What might the following markings on the nail specify?
   Mee's lines _____
   Beau's lines _____
   No moons _____
   Big moons _____
   Lines that run the length of the nail

   _____

2. What do the following shapes of nails suggest to you?
   Scooped nails _____
   Narrow, long nails_____
   Watchglass nails_____

3 . What do the following colors in the fingernails imply?
   Red _____
   Pale _____
   Blue _____
   Pink _____

CHAPTER THREE

THE PALM PROPER

The hand is a visible part of the brain.

— Dr. Charlotte Wolff

Length of the Palm and the Fingers

Traditionally, the length of the palm versus the length of the fingers has meaning. There are many different ways of determining if the fingers are longer than the palm or vice versa. One way is to measure the back of the hand from the wrist bone to the end of the Saturn or longest finger. First measure from the wrist bone to the knuckle at the base of the Saturn (second) finger. This will give you the measurement of the palm. Then measure from the Saturn knuckle to the end of the Saturn finger, the finger of balance on the hand. This will give you the finger measurement. The palm should measure a little longer than the fingers to give balance to the intellectual, emotional and physical facets of the person. If the palm is more than a half inch longer, the fingers are short. If the palm is more than a half inch shorter, the fingers are long.

Short Fingers

Short fingers belong to people who think with their guts. They can be rash in both actions and words, often putting their feet into their mouths. They tend to be impatient and to dislike detailed work. They are usually the ones to make the big plans and let their friends or employees complete the intricate details. Such people will do well in managerial positions where others are working under them.

Long Fingers
Long-fingered people are the thinkers and analysts. They plan everything carefully, sometimes too carefully, often proving themselves bores. They love system and order.

Fingers of Medium Length
The person with medium-length fingers is a thinker and a doer. The owner is balanced between order, direction and completion.

Short Wide Palms
If the palm is short and wide, the person will have a conservative attitude towards life. This person needs physical and emotional security and in order to maintain that security will support the predictabilities and conventionalities of society.

Long Narrow Palms
If the palm is long and narrow (fig. 3.1), the person will be a nervous, moody individual with artistic inclinations. The lines on the palm will help to determine just how neurotic this person might be and if the nervous temperament or neuroses are likely to get in the way of the individual's goals or help to foster them.

As far as compatibility is concerned, people with short palms will understand others with short palms and those with long palms will understand other people with long palms. In business relationships, differences in the palms might prove to be advantageous to both parties: the short-palmed person acting as the anchor, and the narrow-palmed person acting as the artistic influence. In personal relationships, however, the differences between the two shapes might prove to be very frustrating. The short-palmed person could find her companion an eccentric nut, while the narrow, long-palmed person could find her friend a real bore. It would, of course, depend on the total aspects of the palm, both in structure and in the lines, to determine the compatibility of a couple.

As you can see, there are a number of combinations that might occur with the lengths described above, such as a short palm and short fingers, a short palm and long fingers, a long palm and short fingers, and a long palm and long fingers. Fred Gettings classifies the shapes of the palm by these four combinations, referring to them as the four elements: earth, air, fire and water. (I will discuss the shapes of the palm later.)

Arch of the Fingers

The way the fingers are mounted on the palm is important. To be balanced in all areas, the fingers should be evenly set. If the fingers are set in a straight line across the top of the hand, which is rare, you will find a very confident and proud person who, if the other signs in the hand concur, will become a success (fig. 3.2).

Any finger set lower than the normal line reduces the strength of the finger. The two fingers most often found set low on the hand are the Jupiter (index) and Mercury (little) fingers. A low-set Jupiter indicates the self-conscious person, especially if it makes the Jupiter finger appear to be short. If the Jupiter finger is of average length with the low setting, it could be an asset to the individual, otherwise the finger would be of such a length as to suggest a dictatorial nature.

A low-set Mercury finger (fig. 3.3) can show challenges around intimacy. Many people have trouble relating wholly to the people they are sharing their lives with because they are still relating in fashions learned with their own families. Too often, a lover or spouse is reacted to as if that lover or spouse were a parent. Many individuals play the same old games, go through the same old tapes with their mates as they experienced with their own families. Until they can complete the "unfinished business" they have with their parents, sexual adjustments and close relationships will have an unnecessary burden. Full appreciation of the other person means not being tied to the past, not seeing that person behind the mask of some former family connection.

To find out whether the issues are more with the mother or the father, look to the Saturn, or middle Mount. (The Mount is the fleshy, protruding area under each finger.) Saturn is Father Time and will represent the father figure or its polarity, the mother figure. If the Mercury finger is low set and there is a developed Saturn Mount, the unfinished business is more likely with mother. If the mount is flat, the relationship to father needs to be worked on.

Any finger set higher than the normal line increases the importance of the finger which can indicate the qualities of that finger manifest as too much of a good thing (fig. 3.4).

Smooth or Knotty

To determine if your client's fingers are smooth or knotty, run your finger down the side of your client's fingers. If the knuckles are smooth, there will be no resistance. Smooth fingers (fig. 3.5) show a fast thinker who is both intuitive and impulsive. The smoothness shows that there

3.1

3.2

3.3

3.4

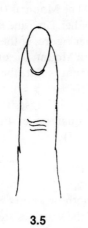

3.5

3.6

is no resistance to the energy flow through the finger. This type of person tends to be easygoing and enjoy being around other people.

Large knuckle formations (fig. 3.6) belong to the person who likes to categorize and classify. The way the person uses these tools will depend upon which knuckle of the finger is developed. If the first phalange of the finger is developed, the person will usually be mentally analytical and like to put things together in her head. This person would make a good scientist, mathematician or inventor. If the second phalange is developed, the person will want to make sure that the environment is orderly, in either home or work. She is the type who knows where everything is and will know if anyone has disturbed her surroundings.

Remember that this is an indication of what the person's psychological makeup is, but you will come across some people who will fight their own nature and will be just the opposite of what their hand traits show. We all have two sides to our nature and the polarity opposite is just a strong indication of this. So don't be discouraged.

Match Them Up #3

1. Low-set Mercury finger _____
2. Fast thinker, intuitive _____
3. Fingers mounted straight across the hand _____
4. Likes to make big plans _____
5. Nervous, moody person _____
6. Low-set Jupiter finger _____
7. Analytical person _____
8. Has conservative attitude toward life _____

A. Long, narrow palm
B. Self-conscious person
C. Short fingers
D. Unfinished issues with parents
E. Short, wide palm
F. Smooth fingers
G. Self-confidence, pride
H. First phalange knuckle development

CHAPTER FOUR

FINGERPRINT PATTERNS

The study of fingerprint patterns, or **dermatoglyphics**, is used by numerous institutions, and has come into use by the medical profession for identifying both physical and mental diseases. It is currently being used in hospitals to spot such birth defects as congenital heart disease and a chromosomal disorder known as Turner's Syndrome. Children born with Turner's Syndrome have one X chromosome, but the second sex chromosome is missing or damaged. Normally, a boy would have an XY set; a girl would have an XX set of sex chromosomes. (For further study of the application of dermatoglyphics, refer to the bibliography at the back of this book.)

There are three types of fingerprint patterns: the arch, the loop and the whorl. These are subdivided into different categories (fig. 4.1).

The fingerprint pattern is formed by a system of parallel ridges and is identified by the number of triadii present. Triadii are made by the triangular-shaped junction of three ridges (fig. 4.2). The most simple print, the arch, has no triadus, with the exception of the tented arch. The loop, the most common of the prints, has one triadus, and the whorl, the most complex print, has two triadii.

The arch pattern occurs most frequently on the Jupiter (index) finger and, according to statistics compiled by Scotland Yard, occurs most often on the left hand. This print, as previously stated, is the most simple pattern and also represents a down-to-earth approach to life. I have found this fingerprint pattern on people whose concerns are to make money in order to enjoy the good things in life. These people are not bothered by others' feelings or opinions and would shock a more refined person with their language. Earthy is the key word to describe people with arches on all their fingers.

In a recent medical study completed at Mount Sinai Hospital in New York, Dr. Mark Swartz has shown a correlation between persons suffering with Mitral Valve Prolapse, which is a variation of the normal rhythm of the heart accompanied with chest pain, and the number of arches present on the fingers and on specific fingers. The pertinence of this study to palmistry is that the arch appeared most often on what we call the Uranus (third) and Mercury (little) fingers. The Uranus finger is traditionally associated with our ability to emotionally cope with people in general. St. Germaine, under his subdivision of mount and illnesses says that the mount of the Sun, which is now referred to as Uranus, "if over developed or excessively lined, shows heart beatings, **aneurism**,...."The Mercury finger is linked with our intimate relationships, such as with our mother, father, husband, wife or lover, and will indicate how we have adjusted to these relationships. In palmistry, emotional or heart problems will show up in this area of our hand, and fingerprint patterns may be just one more gauge to show these physical weaknesses.[3]

The second pattern, known as the loop, makes up approximately 70% of all patterns[4], according to statistics from Scotland Yard. The loop is divided into two distinct patterns: the ulnar loop and the radial loop. The loops are identified by the direction in which they open out on the hand. If the loop opens toward the percussion, it is an ulnar loop. The percussion is the outer side of the hand. If the loop opens toward the thumb, it is a radial loop (fig. 4.3).

The ulnar loop, the most common of the two loops, appears most often on the Mercury finger. People who possess mostly ulnar loops are mild-mannered people who are happy with where they are in life.

A very interesting study conducted by Sardool Singh at the University of New South Wales[5] shows statistically that patients with Down's Syndrome (mongolism), a congenital disease involving the translocation of chromosomes, show greater frequence of ulnar loops on all fingers but the Mercury finger than schizophrenics and mentally retarded males. This Mercury finger, as stated before, is the normal resting

3. Swartz, Mark H., M.D. "Dermatoglyphic Patterns in Patients with Mitral Valve Prolapse: A Clue to Pathogenesis." *The American Journal of Cardiology* 38 (November 4, 1976): 588-92.

4. Cummins, Harold, and Charles Midlo. *Finger Prints, Palms and Soles: An Introduction to Dermatoglyphics*, 68. New York: Dover Publications, 1961.

5. Singh, Sardool. "Dermatoglyphics of Schizphrenics, Patients with Down's Syndrome and Mentally Retarded Males as Compared with Australian Europeans Using Multivariate Statistics." *American Journal of Physical Anthropology* 42 (March 1975): 237-240.

WHORL

LOOP

ARCH

4.1

TRIADUS

4.2

ULNAR LOOP

RACIAL LOOP

ULNAR LOOP

4.3

place for the ulnar loop. The mongoloid child is a very gentle and com-
placent individual. These same adjectives are used to describe the ulnar-
loop personality.

The radial loop is considered in the same vein as the whorl and
basically shows individuality.

The whorl pattern is the most complex pattern and, like the radial
loop, is an indicator of distinction and individuality. There is an old
Chinese formula for fortune-telling that goes as follows:

> One whorl, poor; two whorls, rich
> Three whorls, four whorls, open a pawnshop
> Five whorls, be a go between
> Six whorls, be a thief
> Seven whorls, meet calamities
> Eight whorls, eat chaff
> Nine whorls and one loop, no work to do
> meat till you are old.[6]

There seems to be more truth to this little ditty than meets the eye.
A mixture of loops and whorls, five loops and five whorls, seems to
be the ideal, showing a balanced, healthy person. A person who has
too many whorls will be restless, vacillating, sensitive and clever.

Whorls on all the fingers emphasize the sensitivity of the individual
to such an extent that there may be emotional and mental trauma
associated with too many whorls on the hand. In one study completed
at New South Wales, mentally retarded males compared to patients with
Down's Syndrome had more whorls and radial loops and less ulnar
loops. In the same study, female schizophrenics showed more whorls
and less ulnar loops than the control group.[7]

In the Orient a whorl is considered a good sign showing individuality and creativity associated with the active, male, *yang*, while loops
and arches are associated with the passive, female, *yin*. (According to
Chinese cosmology, *yang* and *yin* are the combination of masculine
and feminine energy forms — masculine or *yang* energy being light,
dry, active and hot; *yin* or feminine energy being passive, dark, cold
and wet. The two combine with each other to produce all that exists
in the universe. When I refer to *yin* and *yang*, I am referring to the
two polar forces of the universe, both of which are needed to complete
the whole, and not to the male or female sex. Both sexes have a

---

6. Cummins, Harold, Ph.D. *Finger Prints, Palms and Soles*, 9. London: Dover Publications, 1961, p.68.
7. Singh, pp. 237-40.

composite of *yin* and *yang* energy.)

The individuality of the whorl can give rise to loneliness because others do not understand the complexity of the person. Such people will just have to learn to stand on their own two feet. The location of the whorl must be taken into consideration. If you were to find this pattern on the thumb (and what a wonderful place to find it), watch out! This person will be a dynamo, someone who will get where he wants to go in a very unusual way. It will again depend on the rest of the hand to determine how he might reach his goals.

A whorl on the Jupiter (index) finger will show a person who will use the ability to lead or teach in a different way. For example, this person might work with retarded or abused children. On the Saturn (second) finger a whorl will show a person whose field of study will have a touch of the eccentric or even the bizarre, maybe the occult!

On Uranus (third finger), this print will show people who will express themselves, in very original ways, *a la* Salvador Dali. On the Mercury (little) finger the whorl will show people who will approach their most intimate relationships and the business/monetary world in unique ways.

One last note: the whorl will act as an asset to any deficiency in a finger, such as a short or low-set finger, or any deficiency in a mount, such as a flat mount.

Test Yourself #4

1. What are the three different kinds of fingerprint patterns?
   A. _____
   B. _____
   C. _____
2. Which fingerprint pattern is the most common? _____
3. Which fingerprint pattern is the most simple?

   _____

4. Which fingerprint pattern is the most complex?

   _____

5. What is the difference between the ulnar and the radial loop?

   _____

6. What one word helps describe the person with all arch patterns?

   _____

   What one word helps describe the person with all loop patterns?

   _____

   What one word helps describe the person with all whorl patterns?

   _____

7 . If you were reading a palm and your client had a short little finger
but had a whorl on that same finger, what would that indicate?

_____

CHAPTER FIVE

THE THUMB AND THE FINGERS
The Thumb

The word **thumb** in Sanskrit means, "He is strong." The thumb is a preaxial (situated in front of the axis of the body) digit which gives freedom of movement and opposition, a quality which separates it from the other fingers of the hand.

In some cultures the thumb is considered such an intricate part of the palm that the palmist reads only this digit to ascertain the makeup of the individual.

The Length of the Thumb
The longer the thumb, the stronger the will of the person and the greater the possibility of achieving her goals.

To be considered of average length, the thumb, when lying next to the fingers, should reach halfway up the third phalange of the Jupiter finger (fig. 5.1). A thumb which reaches the knuckle is considered long (fig. 5.2). A thumb which just reaches the Jupiter finger is considered short (fig. 5.3). This reading would be altered if the thumb itself was set very low in the hand, making the finger appear short when in actuality it is of average length (fig. 5.4).

The person with a long thumb has inner strength and push. She is ruled by the head rather than the heart. She thinks as an individual and does not follow the whims of others. The person with a long, well-shaped thumb will usually be successful.

The short thumb belongs to the person who is ruled by instinct and emotion. The weakness in this thumb comes from the fact that

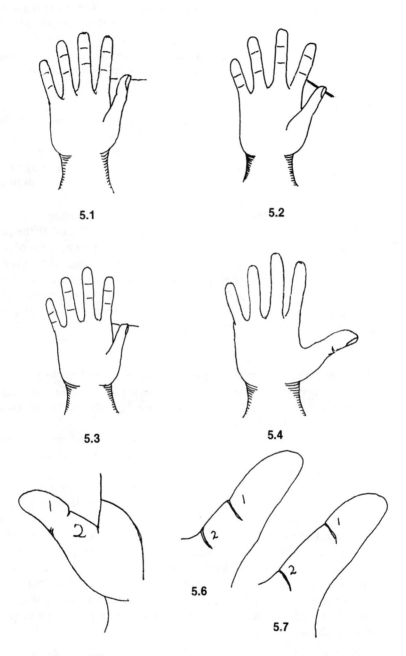

5.1

5.2

5.3

5.4

5.5

5.6

5.7

this person's emotional reactions can cause vacillation in her decision-making abilities. This, however, does not mean that this person cannot become successful. A spur-of-the-moment decision might be just the right one that could put the individual on the road to riches or fame, but another spur-of-the-moment decision could lead to disaster.

Sections

The thumb is divided into two sections. The first phalange, the nail phalange, represents the will and the ability to decide. The second phalange represents judgment and reasoning powers. To be at its best, the two sections should be of equal length, or the nail phalange may be a little shorter than the second phalange (fig. 5.5). This will indicate a balance between thought and action.

If the first phalange is longer than the second phalange, the person will be impulsive (fig. 5.6). She acts before she thinks. If the person has a good head line, knotty fingers or a stiff thumb, some of this impulsiveness will be checked. When the second phalange of the thumb is notably longer than the first phalange, the person will think everything over, and over, and over (fig. 5.7). She will often miss a chance that could have proven to be lucrative due to procrastination. Short or smooth fingers will keep this in check.

Angle

When extended, the thumb opens up into a natural angle from the fingers. The normal angle is between 45° and 60° (fig. 5.8). This angle shows a self-reliant person who is cautious but who is also generous and open to others.

A thumb which is held at a right angle to the fingers shows a lover of liberty and independence. This person is open-minded, generous and needs to be free (fig 5.9).

A thumb which hides itself in the palm can show problems. The will, ego, is in danger. Congenital idiots hold their thumbs in their palms. Epileptics, just prior to a seizure, close their thumb in their palm. Newborn babies conceal their thumbs until they begin to develop.

A hidden thumb shows fear and anxiety. Such people are insecure and hence can be afraid to face their problems. Due to insecurity, they can be overly cautious and suspicious of others. They may not know how to let go and enjoy life, and consequently they suffer. With the help of a competent psychiatrist or counselor, these people can become more realistic.

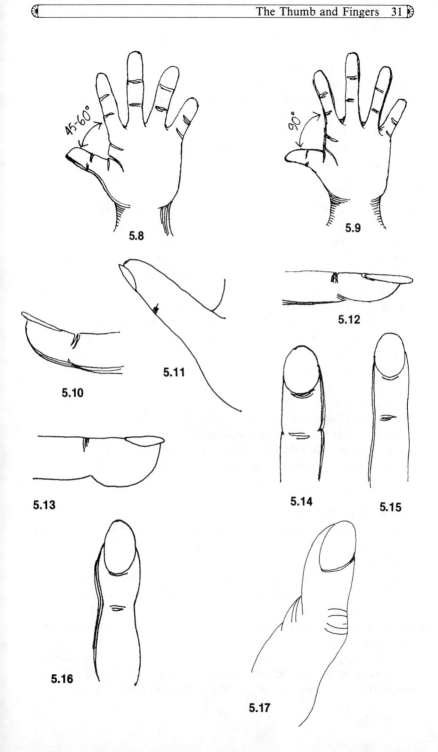

5.8

5.9

5.10

5.11

5.12

5.13

5.14

5.15

5.16

5.17

Supple or Stiff Thumb
The supple thumb (fig. 5.10), or one that bends back easily when touched, shows an adaptable, versatile, easygoing individual. Anywhere is home to this person.

The straight, stiff thumb (fig. 5.11), shows a stubborn, strong-willed and practical person. She is economical and can really be a miser with possessions.

The First Phalange of the Thumb
The flat thumb (fig. 5.12), one that when turned to the side looks like air has been pressed from it, is called the nervous thumb. These people will achieve their goals through excess nervous energy. Even though they do not have a lot of physical vitality and may need rest from time to time to calm their frazzled nerves, these people are survivors. They can find more reserve energy when it is needed than their physically active friends.

The clubbed thumb (fig. 5.13) has been called "the murderers thumb" because it has been found on people capable of extreme fits of anger that have led to physical violence. This thumb is congenital and does not by itself bespeak of crime, but it does show an undercurrent of repressed anger that could lead to violence. We would look for additional clues to support this, such as a ruddy palm which can indicate a hot temper, a distorted Mercury or little finger which can show a violent nature, a developed Upper Mars mount, suggesting an aggressive nature. Just like the Simian line, the emotional tension can be channeled into elevated interests and drives such as sports or artistic/musical areas.

Width of the Thumb
When the thumb is thick throughout (fig. 5.14), it shows good strength and vitality. This person will make things happen out of sheer force if necessary.

The slender, round thumb (fig. 5.15) shows refined logic. These people will get what they want through their ability to wrap others around their fingers. They have the Irish gift of gab and charm. On the negative side, they can be very sly, using others for their own advantage.

The very narrow-waisted thumb (fig. 5.16) shows a tactful, diplomatic person who knows how to handle all people and all situations. However, this person can also be too accommodating.

The Rhythm Knot
The knuckle at the base of the thumb where this digit joins the palm (fig. 5.17), when developed, shows timing ability. Rhythm in all forms can be seen here. This includes playing a musical instrument, dance and the timing of the spoken word used in politics, sales and religion.

The Fingers

Jupiter
In mythology, Jupiter is the king of the gods. He is master of law and philosophy. The Jupiter finger (fig. 5.18), in palmistry, deals with pride, religious feelings, protection and guidance.

When the Jupiter finger is of **average length**, or reaches to the halfway mark of the first phalange of Saturn, then we find a person who tends to realize her potential and feel secure in her own abilities to lead and teach others. Such people do not have to make a big show of themselves to others; the security is within.

If short, the Jupiter finger can indicate a lack of patience with the self and others. The individual may be ego-vulnerable and compensate by being too outspoken, demanding or by giving orders. (I have found short index fingers on many successful salespeople who like to throw their weight around.)

A very long Jupiter finger that is nearly as long as the Saturn finger can show conceit and overconfidence. This can be the finger of the dictator, the person who feels she has so much to offer the world that she forces the world to accept her opinions.

Saturn
In mythology, Saturn is Father Time. In palmistry this (second) finger represents service, duty, restrictions and limitations.

If the finger is of **average length**, that is, one half-tip longer than the Uranus or Jupiter fingers, this shows a sense of balance, of understanding one's duties and services, and the ability to not become overly serious about responsibilities.

If short, there is often an easygoing "I don't care" attitude. This individual may not see the problems that exist in the world and she may be content to coast along having a good time.

A very long Saturn finger can indicate a strong sense of duty and responsibility which might lead to a melancholy and morose attitude toward life. Or, the person could become a recluse in order to get away from responsibilities. The tendency is to be serious.

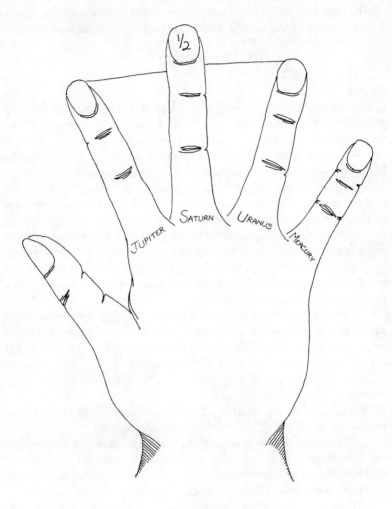

5.18

Uranus
In mythology, Uranus represents the heavens. In palmistry, it represents sociability, public life and aesthetic sense.

If average, the Uranus finger is one half-tip shorter than Saturn. The person has usually adapted to others and to social situations. She can be both warm and sympathetic and appreciates the finer things in life.

If short, the person may shrink away from social activities. She can feel too conspicuous.

If long, it often shows a lover of gambling and notoriety. This is especially true if the mount is developed and the head line is sloping down to the mount of Luna. You will often see a long Uranus finger on actors, actresses and other people who are in the limelight.

Mercury
In mythology, Mercury is the messenger of the gods. In palmistry, this finger deals with communication on all levels — sexual, written and spoken — and deals with our adjustment and adaptability to these forms of communication.

An average Mercury finger will reach to the knuckle of the first phalange of the Uranus finger. These people generally feel comfortable and secure with their ability to express themselves and have adjusted to their relationships with their parents and with the opposite sex. (This, of course, will not be as strong if the Mercury finger is low set in the palm, suggesting some issues still with parents.)

If short, it tends to show a lack of stability and concentration.

A very long Mercury finger may indicate a person who assimilates information so fast, she sometimes misunderstands what was said. This person can be a storyteller and may have linguistic and mimical abilities.

The Phalanges

Each finger, excluding the thumb, should have three distinct and equal sections. If the fingers do not have these distinct areas, the deficient phalange is showing below-average energy and there can be subsequent problems that should be worked on.

I will break down each phalange separately. However, remember, that you will always have to take the entire hand into consideration. Sometimes a deficient section of a finger can help to compensate for an overly-developed trait somewhere else in the palm. It can bring balance into the subject's life, so it is not always a negative aspect. And, depending on the context, certain qualities can be "negative" at one point and "positive" at another.

I will be discussing potential diseases in this section. Let me remind all readers that **disease or health is the choice of the individual. When balanced and dealing with stress in a constructive manner no disease exists.**

Jupiter
Top Phalange: Enjoyment of the beautiful things in life, love of art and music, love of the sensual appetites.

Too Pronounced: Overindulgent in the sensual appetites, appreciates gaudy things. Attracted to the glitter and gold.

Restricted: Problems enjoying life; doesn't know how to take it easy and doesn't believe that she deserves the time off or the fun.

Middle Phalange: Ego, drive, ambition, self.

Too Pronounced: Egocentric, selfish, dictator.

Restricted: Self-effacing.

Lower Phalange: Spiritual transition, idealism, healing, preaching, endings, karmic lessons.

Too Pronounced: Religious fanatic, dreamer, illusions, may get involved in drugs and alcohol.

Restricted: Lack of faith and insight, martyr.

Potential Diseases of Jupiter Finger: Apoplexy, gout, liver malfunctions.

Jupiter issues concern faith. If we are realistic about ourselves and our loved ones and accept ourselves for what we are while working for improvement, then we will not be disillusioned in life but we will be the co-creators in our universe.

Saturn
Top Phalange: Expansion, idealism, teaching, philosophy, travel, foreign people, old people, writing.

Too Pronounced: Looking for perfection, looking for God in self and in others, restless, impulsive.

Restricted: Lack of faith, gives up easily.

Middle Phalange: Work, service, lessons, tradition, stability, security, occupation, father figure.

Too Pronounced: Worrier, nitpicky, puritanical, opinionated.

Restricted: Lack of purpose, close-minded, problem with father figure or authority.

Bottom Phalange: Eccentric, innovative, humanitarian, brotherly love.

Too pronounced: Superficial interactions, will fight for any cause.

Restricted: Not getting involved, antisocial, paranoia.

Potential Diseases of Saturn Finger: Bones, joints, middle/inner ear, bowels and lower stomach.

If you are handling the Saturn issues well — that is, being responsible without carrying everyone's problems on your back and not avoiding your own appropriate responsibilities and duties — then you can bypass problems associated with the Saturn finger.

Uranus

Top Phalange: Communication, teaching, lecturing, writing, curiosity.
Too Pronounced: Difficulty in communicating. Might have communication problem such as dyslexia — a disturbance of the ability to read.
Middle Phalange: Intuitive, motherly, protective, home-oriented, imaginative.
Too Pronounced: Smothering, very emotional, little control over intuitive and psychic ability, fantasies.
Restricted: Insulation, afraid of world, mother figure problems.
Lower Phalange: Ego, creativity, procreation and emotional wellbeing.
Too Pronounced: Egomania, compulsive behavior.
Restricted: Low self-esteem.
Potential Diseases of Uranus Finger: Eyes, backaches, muscles, colds and depression.

In conjunction with Uranus, if you are expressing your innermost negative feelings, such as anger, resentment, fear or frustration in a constructive manner, then many of the problems associated herein can be eliminated.

One way to channel your feelings constructively is by writing in a daily journal or diary. It is a wonderful way to get in touch with who you are and to make it okay to feel your individual emotions rather than repressing them and possibly bringing about disease.

Mercury

Top Phalange: Sexual intensity, investigative, in-depth study.
Too Pronounced: Sexual permissiveness, tears things apart, never appreciative or happy with anything.
Restricted: Sexual-social problems, frigidity, impotency, little insight.
Middle Phalange: Sharing a one-to-one relationship, compromise, receptive, loving, caring, trusting.
Too Pronounced: Difficulty in making up one's mind, can be used, too open and receptive.
Restricted: Not trustworthy, fear of being used.
Bottom Phalange: Investigative, communication, work, service,

responsibility, healing, medicine.

Too Pronounced: Always finding fault, cold.

Restricted: Irresponsible, lets others support and take care of person, problems holding a job.

Potential Diseases of Mercury Finger: Nervous system, sexual organs, reproductive organs and the water system.

With Mercury, it is important that the nervous system be kept in balance so that nervous tension does not control the body. This can be done through meditation, yoga, exercise, hypnosis, relaxation techniques, etc. With respect to the sexual and reproductive areas, examining and facing old ideas about sexual feelings (e.g., guilt built around parents, religion or society) will help to eliminate these problem areas.

Test Yourself #5

1. The average thumb reaches _____ way up the third phalange of the Jupiter finger.
2. A long thumb shows _____.
3. A person with a long thumb might be ruled by her _____.
4. A person with a short thumb might be ruled by her _____.
5. The first section of the thumb represents _____ and _____.
6. The second section of the thumb represents _____ and _____.
7. The thumb that opens in a right angle to the fingers shows _____ .
8. The natural angle of the thumb is between _____ and _____ degrees.
9. A hidden finger implies _____ and _____.
10. The supple thumb suggests an _____, _____, and _____ individual.
11. The straight, stiff thumb can show a _____, strong-willed and _____ person.
12. The flat thumb is called the _____ thumb.
13. The clubbed thumb is called the _____ thumb. Why? _____
14. A very narrow-waisted thumb can indicate a person who is _____ and diplomatic.
15. A developed knuckle at the base of the thumb shows what? _____

16. Name two attributes of the Saturn finger.

    A. _____

    B. _____

17. Which finger deals with communication on all levels? _____.

18. What does the Jupiter finger indicate? _____

19. Which finger, when long, can show a gambler and lover of notoriety? _____

CHAPTER SIX

THE SHAPE OF THE PALM

There are four basic hand shapes: the square palm, the round palm, the philosophical palm and the psychic palm.

The Square Palm

This is also called the useful, practical and earth hand.

Shape
The palm is square and the fingers are usually short and square (fig. 6.1).

Positive Qualities
Uses emotional judgment rather than intelligence, is methodical in habits, punctual, reliable, wants concrete results, has feet on the ground, loves physical actions and loves to work outdoors.

Negative Qualities
Opinionated, possessive, too critical, overly suspicious, is impatient with detailed work. (If the fingers are knotty, the person will be more analytical and less subject to emotional decisions.)

Occupations
Medicine, law, science, business, farming, astrologer.

EARTH HAND

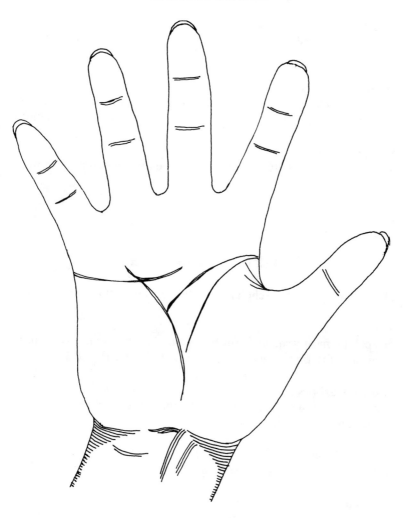

6.1

The Round Palm

This is also called the conic, creative and fire hand.

Shape
The palm is round and the fingers are usually short with rounded tips (fig. 6.2).

Positive Qualities
Warm, sociable, artistic, sensitive, loves music and the performing arts, is in constant need of excitement and activity, aesthetic appreciation.

Negative Qualities
Impulsive, rash, moody, exhibitionist, egocentric, does not finish what is started.

Occupations
Dancer, actor, artist.

The Philosophical Hand

This is also called the scholarly, spatulate, intellectual or air hand.

Shape
The palm is mostly square in shape but a bit longer than the true square palm, and the fingers are long and usually knotty (fig. 6.3).

Positive Qualities
Has good reasoning abilities, is logical, diplomatic, kindhearted, quick-witted, discriminating.

Negative Qualities
A perfectionist, a stick-in-the-mud.

Occupations
Professor, judge, minister, historian, statesman, inventor.

The Psychic Hand

This is also called the sensitive, spiritual or water hand.

FIRE HAND

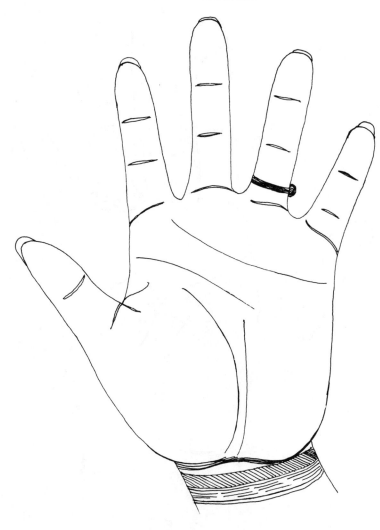

6.2

AIR HAND

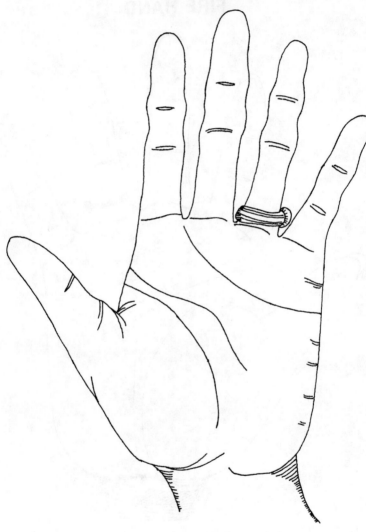

6.3

Shape
The palm is long and narrow and the fingers are long and unusually tapered at the ends (fig. 6.4).

Positive Qualities
Contemplative, poetic, artistic, intuitive and spiritual.

Negative Qualities
Nervous, high strung, overly sensitive, neurotic, lives in the clouds.

Occupations
Dancer, poet, writer artist, mystic, hermit.

Diseases Which Can Show in the Palm

The following information shows how the palm indicates health problems due to such things as improper diet, stress, inherent sensitivities, etc. Any potential problem would need to be confirmed by other indicators and is only a warning to us to pay better attention to our bodies — physically, mentally, emotionally and spiritually. Each of you needs to find the paths best suited to you as a unique human being to maintain your health goals. For example, I work out at a gym and meditate. Another friend of mine does yoga and uses science of the mind techniques for positive thinking. Another friends does not do any of this, but keeps healthy because of his positive mental outlook and because he does not believe in disease.

Alcoholism
This problem can be suggested by a deficient Jupiter finger or an interference line (coming from either the Life line or a Mars line), ending in a star on the Mount of Luna (fig. 6.5).

Arthritis
This can be implied by ruddy palms with swelling of the knuckles at the base or the tips of the fingers. Ruddy palms can also indicate high blood pressure and gout.

Cancer and Diabetes
According to palmist Myrah Lawrance, one can detect cancer and diabetes in one's immediate family by specific ingrained patterns in the texture of the skin. The patterns will be found between the Uranus and the Mercury fingers in the quadrangle (the area between the head and

WATER HAND

6.4

the heart line), and can sometimes be found as far down as the Mount of Luna. A raised whorl in the skin texture, circular in formation, like a fingerprint pattern, shows the possibility of cancer in the immediate family (fig. 6.6).

Studies suggest that many cancer patients experience feelings of hopelessness and/or anger, never expressed, before the onset of the disease. There is often a severe, subjective loss preceding the onset of the cancer. Learning to express negative emotions in a constructive fashion is important. The channels of expression are as unique as each individual person and can include acting, directing, writing, dancing, drawing, sculpting, playing a musical instrument, support from friends, etc. Don't hold on. Getting feelings out and then forgiving is valuable. Often the biggest challenge is forgiving ourselves.

A mark like a horseshoe (fig. 6.6) can show the possibility of diabetes or kidney disease in the immediate family. I have verified both of these markings in my readings. You can find out if the sensitivity to this disease might exist for your client by looking at his Mercury (little) finger. A bend in the upper phalange of this finger (fig. 6.7) can indicate problems with the kidneys, bladder or diabetes.

These problems are sometimes tied to a fear of allowing anyone to get too close. Intimacy can seem like a threat, where you might get hurt. On a deeper level, there can be an issue of faith in yourself. Counseling or therapy can help to work this out, or other avenues to learning to trust another human being.

Female Problems
These can include problems conceiving and diseases of the uterus and/or ovaries. Such can be suggested by an elevated Luna Mount (fig. 6.8) with an undeveloped mount of Venus, both with many lines, and a Life line which dips abruptly towards the lower part of the Luna Mount. If the lower phalange of Mercury appears puffy or thick, then the ovaries may be indicated.

Reproductive problems can mirror inner ambivalence or confusion about the female role, or guilt around sexuality. Facing the mixed feelings and expressing them can be helpful. Clarifying one's goals and values around sex is useful. Counseling can assist in working through guilt and sorting one's own responses from what other people have taught and said we are supposed to do and feel.

Glandular Disturbances
Person suffering from glandular disturbances affecting their sexual development will often have a short little finger (fig. 6.9).

High-strung Person
A nervous, high-strung person will often have a palm with many fine, spidery lines that crisscross the hand in all directions, making it very difficult to read. The palm will usually be long and narrow (fig. 6.10) and is what Fred Gettings would term "the water hand."

If a person is uncomfortable with their nervousness, learning to float, to detach, to be a spectator may be helpful. People can utilize meditation, relaxation techniques, biofeedback, hypnosis and other tools if they desire.

Mongoloids
Mongoloids have both short thumbs and short Mercury fingers and will usually have a Simian line (fig. 6.11), technically a running together of the heart and the head line. (This will be discussed at length later in the book.)

If you are concerned about your own physical health, please visit your own family doctor before diagnosing a disease.

Combination Hands

It is rare that you find a hand that is one shape only. We all possess a combination of signs and traits. That is what makes us interesting as individuals and also provides tension aspects in our personality makeup. Each aspect has to be worked with. We have to integrate the parts in order to develop the whole, otherwise we deny a part of ourselves and thus cause psychological/emotional problems.

How can you know when a person has a combination hand? There are many ways to read the different signs:

One — The Fingertips
Are the fingertips square (earth), spatulate (air), round (fire) or psychic (water)? If you have a combination of two, then you have to discuss the different qualities of same and, in most cases, a tension aspect.

For instance, the square nail and the round nail. One aspect (square) talks about security, about practical and realistic results, while the round nail talks about freedom, curiosity, etc. There is opposition here. One side of the personality wants one thing and one wants another thing. Both have to be integrated. You might say that it is impossible, but that is not so. This individual could, for instance, get into advertising, a field that can incorporate both the creative, expressive, free-loving side and the practical, realistic side (there is a paycheck and set

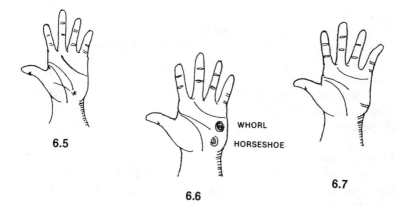

6.5

6.6

WHORL

HORSESHOE

6.7

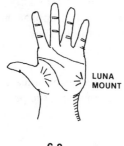

LUNA
MOUNT

6.8

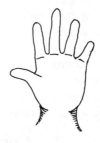

6.9

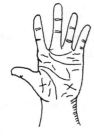

6.10

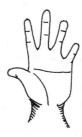

6.11

hours). Both sides are worked on.

Two — The lines

The earth and fire hands have the strongest lines. The difference is that the earth hand has the major lines with few ancillary lines, while the fire hand has a network of lines, showing its excitable and creative character.

The air and water hands have the lighter lines, with the water hand usually having many crisscross lines, indicating its nervous temperament.

Three — Finger lengths

The earth and fire hands have the shorter fingers, showing impulsive, quick, forceful natures. The air and water hand have the longer fingers, indicating ability for patience and weighing of an issue.

The way to tell the air finger from the water finger is by the knotty formation of the scholarly hand, showing its analytical approach in contrast to water, which is intuitive and just lets things flow.

Four — The mounts

The mounts (which will be discussed in a later chapter) also indicate element predominance. If the water mounts are predominant, the person has more water characteristics, and so on.

Combinations

Earth and Fire
Here we have the steamroller. This person can be overwhelming. They go full steam ahead and everyone had better get out of the way.

Earth and Water
Earth gets water moving, gives it direction. Water calms earth down and makes earth slower in its actions and reactions.

Earth and Air
Here we have the driving force of earth pushing the air along and making concrete use of air's ideas.

Fire and Water
The fire and water create steam, which results in strong emotional power and intensity. The fire acts as the creative stimulus and the water conducts.

Fire and Air
A complementary combination. Fire is the initiator, the driving force; air is the thinking force. Air keeps the pure fire person from being rash and makes fire use its power constructively. A good sense of humor is indicated by this combination.

Air and Water
Air spurs water along, gives it a channel to express itself. Water's intuitive and inspired nature gives air a lot of new ideas.

Let's do a few hands. Look at **Example A** (fig. 6.12). Finger endings are round, so we have fire. The palm and the lines are basically earthy but the palm shape is fire. We have a combination of an earth and a fire hand — a steamroller.

This woman is a Capricorn, which is an earth sign. She has a lot of fire elements in her personality. She is an account manager and is usually causing discord by opening her mouth when she shouldn't.

Example B (fig. 6.13). Obviously a much more nervous hand. This is a water/air hand. The palm is long and rectangular with long fingers showing the elements of air. The fingers are knotty (although this is not clear in the illustration), so we have air fingers with lines that are definitely water. (Notice the fish symbol on the palm — across from the thumb on what is called the Mount of Luna.) This gentleman is a Scorpio, a water sign. He is a commercial artist.

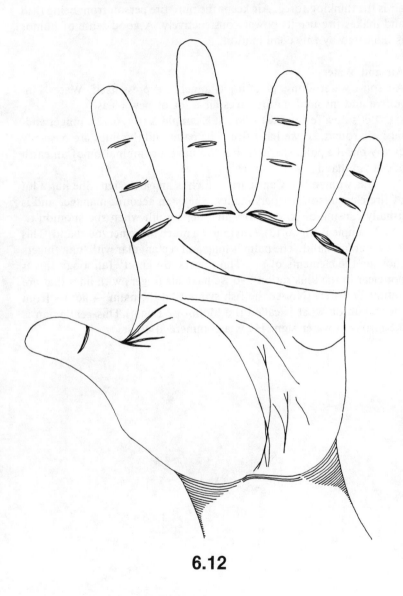

6.12

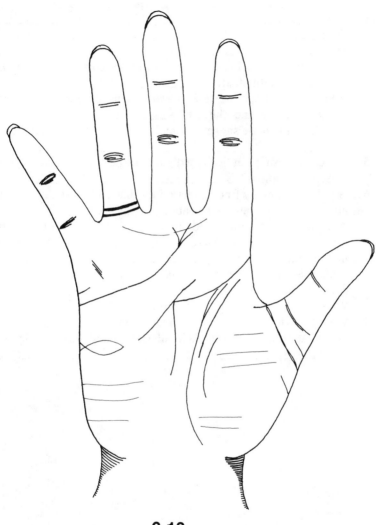

6.13

Test Yourself #6

1. Name the four major shapes of the hand.
   A. _____
   B. _____
   C. _____
   D. _____
2. Which of the four hand shapes indicates the most sensitive and high-strung individual? _____
3. Which hand shape indicates a warm, sensitive person who appreciates music and the arts? _____
4. Which hand shape suggests someone reliable and punctual?
   _____
5. Which hand shape indicates a diplomatic person who shows good reasoning abilities? _____
6. A palm with many fine, spidery lines that crisscross the hand in all directions suggests what about the person? _____
7. A horseshoe mark ingrained in the palm at the quadrangle in the area of the Uranus and Mercury fingers might imply what disease in the immediate family? _____
8. Ruddy palms with swelling at the knuckles at the base of the fingers might indicate what? _____
   What can the individual do about it? _____
9. What markings might show female problems? _____
   and what could she do to help alleviate/avoid such problems?
   _____

CHAPTER SEVEN

MOUNTS, DISPLACEMENTS AND MARKINGS

The lines that make prints in the hand are laid down in the fifth week of pregnancy. And they never change. It's possible they could have a coupling with some psychological characteristics influenced by heredity.

— J. A. Gengerelli
Statistician from U.C.L.A.

The mounts of Jupiter, Saturn, Uranus and Mercury are located under each of the corresponding fingers, while the mounts of Upper Mars, Lower Mars, the Plain of Mars, Luna, Pluto, Neptune, Venus and the Sun are located as developed areas in the palm proper (fig. 7.1).

The mounts are a source of energy showing potential attributes and talents. The mount, to be considered balanced, should be firm to the touch and developed. By that I mean the mount should not be completely flat or mushy when you touch it. If flat, do not despair. It is just indicating that you are not using the full potential of that mount. The energy can be stimulated by a change in attitudes, lifestyle, etc. If the mount is overdeveloped, it shows a potential for overindulgence in the specific qualities represented therein. (An overdeveloped mount extends far higher than the other mounts in the hand.) You can harness the energy herein and channel it into constructive areas. Otherwise, you may overdo the expression of that energy.

The mounts of Jupiter, Saturn, Uranus and Mercury can be easily found by locating what is called the apex design. Four such designs create the mount location. The triangle in the middle of the apex design

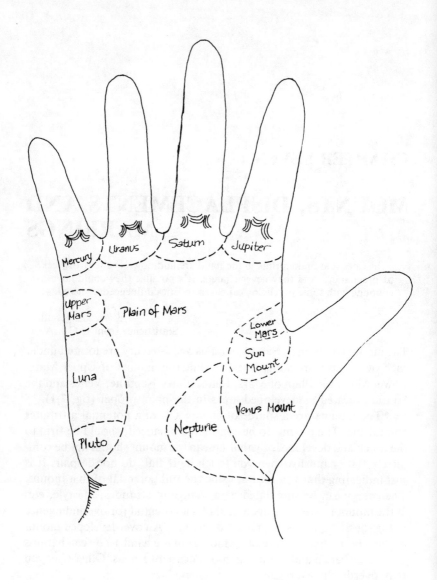

7.1

is the center of the mount (fig. 7.1). For the mount to be at its best, it should be directly under the finger associated with it.

The other mounts are discernible by location and usually take some practice and patience to recognize.

The Jupiter Mount

The Mount of Jupiter is located in the active, conscious zone, and, when developed, shows diplomacy, pride, leadership, ambition and religious qualities. If the Mount of Jupiter is flat, the person may lack self-respect and pride and might take a back seat due to her lack of self-confidence. (This would be adjusted if the person has a good thumb and a whorl on the Jupiter finger.) If the mount is overdeveloped — especially if the person has a long Jupiter finger — we find someone who has leadership qualities, someone who enjoys authority and power, and who could prove to be overbearing, a dictator, expecting everyone to conform to her ideas.

The mount must be taken into consideration along with the finger and its attributes. If the Jupiter finger is of normal length and the mount is centered, developed and firm, these people will tend to be proud, ambitious, feel confident to lead others, have deep religious feelings and, if the other signs in the hand concur, achieve their goals.

If the mount of Jupiter is developed but the Jupiter finger is short, the individuals may not want to be leaders in the conventional manner but will generally be dynamic individuals with the ability to express themselves. If, on the other hand, the Mount of Jupiter is flat and the Jupiter finger is short, such people might not exert themselves because of their own poor self-images.

Seldom, however, will you find the mounts where they should be, so let us look at the displaced Jupiter Mount.

Displacement of the Jupiter Mount
If the Mount of Jupiter is displaced towards the Saturn finger, the person is likely to be self-conscious, thoughtful and more serious in nature than the pure Jupiterian.

If the mount is displaced towards the heart line, this person's pride often centers around the affections.

If the mount is displaced towards the head line, the person will usually be proud of the intellect, but could also be arrogant, thinking she knows it all.

Markings on Jupiter

A **square** on the Jupiter Mount (fig. 7.2) has been called the **Teacher's Square** and shows the ability to express one's thoughts to others. The teaching does not have to be in the conventional classroom sense. I have often found this mark on the hands of persons teaching in the metaphysical field.

A **triangle** (fig. 7.3) shows unusual diplomacy and tact, stressing the ability to deal with the world in a political sense.

A **star** (fig. 7.4) indicates great ambition, which usually leads to success. It can show a happy or wealthy marriage for either sex.

A **grille** (fig. 7.5) shows a need to lead others and to have authority, but the power could be as a dictator.

A **cross** (fig. 7.6) traditionally means a happy union, but I have not yet confirmed this.

A **circle** (fig. 7.7), which is a rare mark, shows the potential of success.

A **vertical line** is a positive sign and enhances the good qualities of the Jupiter Mount, while **a horizontal line** may indicate a barrier to the energies of the mount and will have to be overcome (fig. 7.8).

The Ring of Solomon (fig. 7.9), a very favorable sign, shows the ability to influence others due to the intellectual and intuitive understanding of oneself and of others.

The Ring of Solomon and the Teacher's Square are often considered spiritual signs on the hand and show a potential for elevating oneself.

The Saturn Mount

The Mount of Saturn is located in the active zone and lies both in the conscious and the unconscious zone of the hand, dividing the two zones into the appropriate areas. When this mount is developed, we often find a studious and philosophical person who is serious about life and the duties that come with life.

If the Mount of Saturn is flat, the person will not usually worry about life's difficulties and thus appear far calmer than a true Saturnian friend with a developed mount. People with flat Saturn mounts seldom worry about what tomorrow may bring.

When the Saturn Mount is overdeveloped, we find a danger of an imbalance between the conscious and the unconscious mind. This person has a tendency to overanalyze everything, thus becoming too sensitive to the world and its problems. She may appear misanthropic when in fact she is just the opposite.

JUPITER

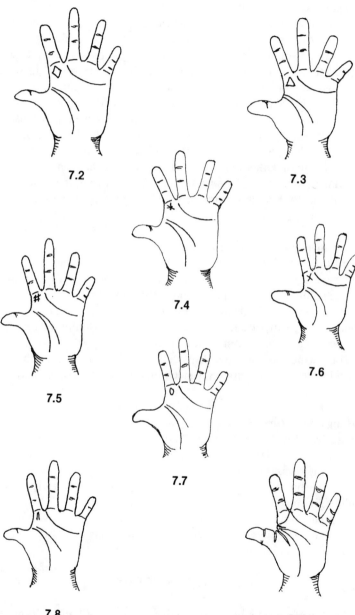

7.2

7.3

7.4

7.5

7.6

7.7

7.8

7.9

Persons with developed Saturn mounts do well as scientists, farmers, philosophers, psychologists, musicians (since this mount deals with balance and harmony, also components of music) and as students or teachers of the occult.

When the Mount of Saturn is developed and there is a good Saturn finger, we have someone who is interested in studies and who is interested in finding the why and wherefore to philosophical and scientific questions. This person has the ability to function well in social situations, but does not need to have people about in order to be happy.

When the Saturn finger is long and the Mount of Saturn is overdeveloped, the person is usually extremely sensitive to world issues and problems. Such people may become so miserable because of their sensitivities that they could estrange themselves from others in order to cope. If, on the other hand, the Saturn finger is short and the owner has a flat Saturn Mount, the person may be too easygoing. She might find it difficult to complete any task, always finding something better to do at the moment.

Displacement of the Saturn Mount
If the Mount of Saturn is displaced towards Jupiter, the people will often have some of the pride and self-confidence from the Jupiter Mount spilling into their duties and responsibilities.

If the mount is displaced towards Uranus, some of the introverted tendencies of Saturn are lifted, and this person is usually warmer and more sociable than the pure Saturnian.

If the Mount of Saturn is displaced towards the heart line, the person could overanalyze emotional encounters and be apprehensive about them.

Markings on Saturn
One **vertical line** on Saturn (fig. 7.10) means financial security.

A **triangle** on Saturn (fig. 7.11) shows aptitude for serious studies, often in the occult arts or in religious fields.

A **circle** on the Saturn Mount (fig. 7.12) shows an aptitude for the occult, religious area.

A **grille** on the Saturn Mount (fig. 7.13) shows a tendency to brood and to find something wrong with everything. This can also indicate a good organizer, planner or efficiency expert.

The Uranus Mount

The Mount of Uranus lies in the active zone of the hand. Uranus is

SATURN

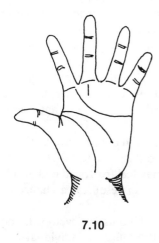

7.10

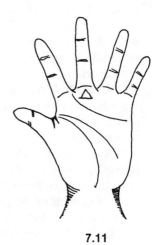

7.11

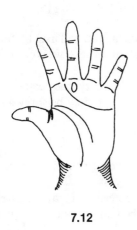

7.12

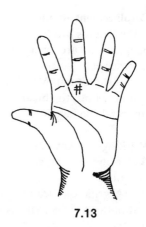

7.13

the first finger to fall directly into the unconscious zone, making its qualities less direct, but just as strong. If this mount is developed, you will generally find a person who enjoys people, who is sociable, loves novelty, the eccentric, and who is often a lover and proprietor of art.

A person with a flat Uranus Mount may feel uncomfortable in most social situations because she does not possess the security and grace to handle the position of being different in any way. She is often too self-conscious.

When the Mount of Uranus is overdeveloped, we can find a person who has a unique personality which draws others to her, but who could prove to be overbearing with a need to be the constant center of attention.

A person who has a flat Uranus Mount and a short Uranus finger is usually a very retiring human being who does not feel that she has anything to offer the world. Such people may feel frustrated and unfulfilled because they do not give their talents or resources a chance to meet the test of life.

If, on the other hand, the Mount of Uranus is developed, the Uranus finger is long and there is a good thumb, the individual will often perform a job, no matter what area it may be in, to impress others and for adulation.

If the person possesses a good Mount of Uranus and a long Uranus finger but has a short thumb, the person may have a weak will and be subject to the influence of others. This can be the mark of the gambler.

Displacement of the Uranus Mount

If the Uranus Mount is displaced towards Saturn, you will usually find people who are protective of children and of others weaker than themselves.

If the Uranus Mount is displaced towards Mercury, the person can combine both the business and creative worlds and may be shrewd in financial management and use of talents.

Markings on Uranus

A **star** on the Uranus Mount (fig. 7.14) shows the possibility of success and fame.

A **grille** on Uranus (fig. 7.15) shows the need to be appreciated and noticed. This mark is often found on the hands of actors, opera singers, etc.

A **triangle** on Uranus (fig. 7.16) shows that the individual is an inspired craftsperson who, if the other signs concur, will become successful.

URANUS

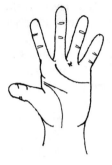

7.14

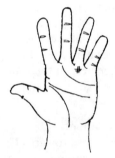

7.15

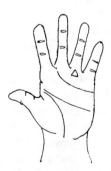

7.16

The Mercury Mount

The Mount of Mercury is in the active, unconscious zones of the hand and, when developed, deals with communication on all levels. It shows eloquence, shrewdness and aptitude for the occult, medicine and science. The Mercurian mind is quick with comprehensive understanding.

If the mount is flat, the person will not usually be interested in either the business world or the world of medicine. The practical mind may be less developed with the individual inclined to abstractions or flights of fancy.

If the Mount of Mercury is overdeveloped, it shows signs of ambition and shrewdness in obtaining goals. This is especially true if the Mercury finger is crooked (fig. 7.17). This person has the gift of gab and knows how to take advantage of every situation.

A very long Mercury finger with a good firm Mercury Mount shows someone who can communicate easily, with eloquence, and who knows how to approach others. Many politicians have this winning combination. If the top (nailed) phalange on Mercury is long, it tends to indicate linguistic abilities.

If the Mount of Mercury is flat and the Mercury finger is short, this suggests someone who does not have a lot of business know-how. These individuals may put their feet in their mouths because they do not think before they speak.

Displacement of the Mercury Mount
If the Mount of Mercury is displaced towards Uranus, there is a blend of business with art. This combination is seen on the hands of politicians, lawyers and religious leaders who use their creative communication abilities in a business sense.

Markings on Mercury
Three **vertical lines** on Mercury (fig. 7.18) indicate healing ability in either the medical world or in the psychic world.

A **star** on the Mount of Mercury (fig 7.19) shows a talent for science or business.

A **grille** on Mercury (fig. 7.20) shows shrewdness and extreme nervousness.

A **triangle** on Mercury (fig. 7.21) shows a love of mimicry.

A **cross** on Mercury (fig. 7.22) can indicate an overly accommodating nature. Such people might often use the polite lie to avoid confrontations.

MERCURY

7.17

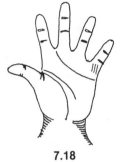

7.18

7.19

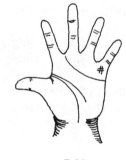

7.20

7.21

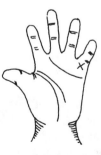

7.22

The Upper Mars Mount

Upper Mars, also referred to as passive Mars, lies in the unconscious zone of the hand and, if firm and developed, represents endurance and instinctive bravery. This is always a good mount to have developed since it adds the desire to survive all of life's obstacles.

If this mount is flat, you will find a person who would rather not put up with life's irritations and who may approach situations with fear and apprehension. This type of person should deal with fears and anxieties in a responsible manner. A partner can help the individual in this endeavor.

If this mount is overdeveloped, it could show a rather daring and rash individual who might become a hero posthumously.

Displacement of Upper Mars
If Upper Mars is displaced towards Mercury, the person usually has fortitude and pluck.

If Upper Mars is displaced towards the Plain of Mars (fig. 7.1), the fighting field, the person may be aggressive.

If Upper Mars is displaced towards Luna, the person has charismatic and persuasive abilities.

Markings on Upper Mars
A vertical line on Upper Mars (fig. 7.23) shows constant irritation. The excessive energy can be channeled into sports.

A grille on Upper Mars (fig. 7.24) shows a tendency for holding in anger. Again, the person should have a physical outlet such as dancing, running or sports.

A horizontal line on Upper Mars (fig. 7.25) indicates the possibility of enemies due to the owner's temper and irritability. The subject might make a great investigator.

The Luna Mount

The Mount of Luna is in the passive, unconscious zones of the hand and, when developed, emphasizes the unconscious, imagination, creativity and the occult.

A person who has a flat mount of Lune can be an unimaginative soul who will tend to find any Lunarian friends a little bizarre even though she might find them exciting.

An overdeveloped Mount of Luna can indicate an overactive imagination. Coupled with restlessness, this could show the possibility of

UPPER MARS

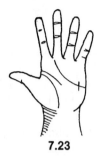

7.23

7.24

7.25
LUNA

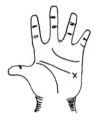

7.26

7.27

7.28

mental and emotional instability. Hopefully, if you were to find this combination in someone's hand, you would find some other redeeming qualities — a good, strong thumb or a developed passive Mars — showing some endurance to put up with life and keep her on solid ground.

Displacement of the Luna Mount

If the Mount of Luna is displaced towards Upper Mars, we generally find a person with a controlled imagination.

If the Mount of Luna is displaced towards the percussion, we find a person whose restlessness will usually be more on the physical level, showing a need to travel.

If the Mount of Lune is displaced towards the palm proper, the person's imagination might increase her aggressive nature.

Markings on Luna

A **cross** on Luna (fig. 7.26) shows a very active imagination.

A **triangle** on Luna (fig. 7.27) shows a gift of prophecy or intuition.

A **grille** on Luna (fig. 7.28) shows an overactive imagination which might bring on a lot of worrying.

The Pluto Mount

Pluto is located at the bottom of the Mount of Luna and is in the unconscious, passive zones of the palm. This planet in astrology is the planet of life, death and of regeneration.

If Pluto is developed, it emphasizes the power of the imagination, of creation and, due to its location in the hand, has a connection with the ancient mysteries.

If Pluto is flat, the person might still be creative, but her energy might not include or take into consideration the occult or metaphysical world.

Markings on Pluto

A **triangle** on Pluto (fig. 7.29) would only add to the powers of imagination and creativity in the occult field.

A **grille** on Pluto (fig. 7.30) could indicate misuse of the inherent psychic powers. The person needs to develop her own inner security and learn how to deal with the power issues in a constructive manner. That can be accomplished through teaching in competitive fields, sports, business or games.

PLUTO

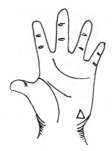

7.29

7.30

The Neptune Mount

The Neptune Mount lies at the bottom of the hand between Luna and Venus. Like Saturn, it represents the dividing line between the conscious and the unconscious zones of the hand, but unlike Saturn, which is in the active zone, Neptune lies in the passive zone and is indirect, instinctive and mysterious. (Sounds fascinating, doesn't it?) Neptune represents hypnotic qualities, enchantment, and possible camouflage and deception.

When the mount is developed, it shows a person who has the power to mesmerize an audience. Hopefully, the other markings in the palm will be of a constructive nature, otherwise this person could use these powers in a destructive manner (e.g., Hitler). The flat mount of Neptune does not mean that the person will be unable to communicate. A good Mercury Mount and Mercury finger would show speaking ability. A flat mount of Neptune merely shows that the person may take a back seat to someone else.

Markings on Neptune
If you were to find the markings of a circle, a star, or a triangle on Neptune, you can be assured that these add intuitive, artistic and musical talent to the mount.

If, however, you were to find markings of a cross or grille, there are lessons indicated with illusion, and possibly drug or alcohol problems. The subject needs to channel energy into helping other people through possibly counseling for the Alcoholics Anonymous or a drug rehabilitation program, etc.

The Venus Mount

The Venus Mount, named after the goddess of love and beauty, lies in the active but unconscious zone of the hand and, when developed, shows a warm, emotionally giving person who possesses physical prowess.

If the Mount of Venus is flat, the person is usually more of an intellectual who feels with the head rather than with the heart. This can make the individual appear cold. You will have to look at her Heart line to determine if this person is really selfish or simply someone who does not emote.

If the Mount of Venus is overdeveloped, you will tend to find someone who is into the sensual pleasures of life. This person is usually on the move due to an abundance of physical energy. Salespeople, dancers and athletes generally have a well-developed Mount of Venus.

If the thumb is well-developed and the Mount of Venus is developed, you are often in the presence of a dynamo of energy who would do great in public relations. She would not enjoy an 8-to-5 office job. She does not want to sit still that long. If the thumb is long and developed, but the Mount of Venus is flat, the person will have the drive to accomplish all goals, but will often prefer a job where she is not continuously in the public's eye. She may not have the emotional energy to cope with people on a constant basis. She generally does best in research work where she has time away from other people.

A person with a developed Mount of Venus but with a short thumb may be someone who could handle the routine 8-to-5 job. She tends to do best with definite objectives and a certain amount of time to complete those objectives. This type of person can handle the public but usually has no desire to be in a managerial position.

Displacement of the Venus Mount
If Venus is displaced towards the thumb, the emotions may rule the will.

If the Mount of Venus is displaced toward the wrist, the owner will generally be a sensuous, physical person.

Markings on Venus
A grille on Venus (fig. 7.31) can show an excess need for love and affection. The strength or weakness of the sections of the thumb will show whether the person might put herself into a dangerous position due to an excessive need for love and attention.

A cross on the Venus Mount, not touching the Life line (fig. 7.32), can show a close encounter in one's own life or a severe emotional or physical illness.

A cross on the outside of the Life line (fig. 7.33) which touches the line shows the loss of a loved one or the sickness of someone close to the client.

Horizontal lines that cross the Mount of Venus (fig. 7.34), which either do or do not go through the Life line onto the palm proper are referred to as worry or interference lines and show a person who may allow worries or outside influences to sap her energy.

Lines that run parallel to the Life line but which are lighter in density than the major line (fig. 7.35) are referred to as **influence lines**. They are indicators of people in the owner's life who have had considerable influence on that individual.

The **line of Mars**, or sister line (fig. 7.36), is a parallel line to the Life line and is as dark in density as the line of life. It is sometimes called

VENUS

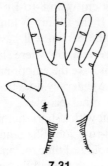

7.31

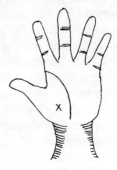

7.32

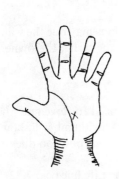

7.33

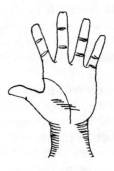

7.34

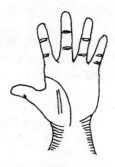

7.35

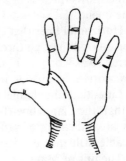

7.36

the "antibody line" and is usually found present for the period of time that the Life line is either badly islanded or broken, showing protection and strength for the individual during times of stress.

The Sun Mount

The Mount of the Sun lies below the second joint of the thumb and is in the conscious, passive zone of the palm.

When this mount is developed, it indicates success through push and will.

If overdeveloped, this person could be a blowhard, someone who needs to be praised continually.

A flattened Sun Mount shows a person who might be insecure and could need a push to keep going.

Markings on the Sun

A **star** or **triangle** (fig. 7.37) on this mount enhances the chances for success through drive. If excessive, ambition could be a problem.

A **grille** (fig. 7.38) shows interference due to worry and anxieties. Again, the subject has a lot of energy that could be channeled towards a successful career.

The Lower Mars Mount

Lower Mars Mount is in the active, conscious zone of the hand and when developed shows initiative, ambition, courage and fight.

If the Mount of Lower Mars is flat, you will tend to find someone who does not care for arguments, someone who will back off when cornered, and someone who has to be pushed to complete a task. (Of course, a good, long thumb with the first phalange being well-developed would counterbalance this.)

If the Mount of Lower Mars is overdeveloped, we may find someone who would rather punch than listen. Here is the born fighter whose temper could prove to be overbearing. Or, they could make a great boxer or athlete.

Displacement of Lower Mars Mount

If Lower Mars is displaced towards the Jupiter Mount, it shows the power of initiative and ambition due to personal dignity and pride.

If Lower Mars is displaced towards Venus, we have the power of endurance and courage due to affections.

SUN

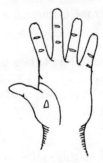

7.37

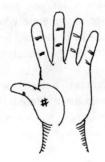

7.38

Markings on Lower Mars

A vertical line on Lower Mars (fig. 7.39) would indicate courage and aggressiveness.

A grille on Lower Mars (fig. 7.40) can show a tendency to quarrel and that the owner possessed an aggressive nature.

A cross on Lower Mars (fig. 7.41) would show the potential of a person who tends to lose control of her temper.

A star on Lower Mars (fig. 7.42) can show a person who will fight against all obstacles to obtain her goals.

Test Yourself #7

1. Name the mounts.

   _____

   _____

   _____

2. How do you identify a mount? _____

3. Which mounts are in the active part of the hand? _____

4. Which mounts are in the passive parts of the hand? _____

   _____

5. What does the Jupiter Mount represent? _____

6. A square on Jupiter is called the _____ and shows what? _____

7. The Ring of Solomon is found where and indicates what? ____

   _____

8. What does the Saturn Mount represent? _____

9. Persons with developed Saturn Mounts usually do well in what occupations? _____

10. A grille on the Saturn Mount shows a tendency to _____.

11. What are the qualities of the Uranus Mount? _____

12. The markings of a potential gambler are what? _____

    _____

13. If the Uranus Mount is displaced towards Mercury, what two attributes might your client combine into one?

    _____ and the _____ worlds.

14. A triangle on Uranus implies what? _____

15. A grille on Uranus suggests what? _____

16. What are the qualities of the Mercury Mount? _____

    _____

LOWER MARS

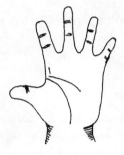

7.39

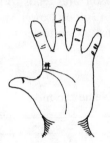

7.40

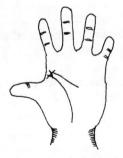

7.41

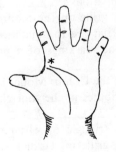

7.42

17. Three vertical lines on Mercury could indicate _____ ability in either the medical world or in the psychic world.

18. A triangle on Mercury denotes what? _____ _____

19. What qualities are associated with Upper Mars? _____

20. If Upper Mars is overdeveloped, what might it indicate? _____ _____

21. A grille on Upper Mars shows a tendency for what ailment? And what options might the person pursue to keep or regain good health? _____

22. A horizontal line on Upper Mars shows the possibility of what? _____

23. What qualities are associated with the Luna Mount? _____

24. An overdeveloped Luna Mount can show what? _____

25. If the Luna Mount is displaced toward the palm proper, we might find what? _____

26. A grille on Luna might indicate an _____ .

27. What qualities are associated with the Pluto Mount? _____

28. A grille on Pluto could indicate misuse of what? _____

29. What are the qualities of the Neptune Mount? _____

30. What does the Venus Mount represent? _____

31. A grille on Venus could show what? _____

32. A cross on the Venus Mount, not touching the Life line shows what? _____

33. A cross on the outside of the Life line touching the line suggests what? _____

34. Light, parallel lines to the Life line on the Venus Mount show what? _____

35. What is the line of Mars? _____

36. What does the Sun Mount represent? _____

37. If the Sun Mount is overdeveloped, what might you find? _____ _____

38. A grille on the Sun Mount shows what? _____

39. What are the qualities of Lower Mars? _____

40. A cross on Lower Mars could indicate what? _____

CHAPTER EIGHT

THE MAJOR LINES IN THE HAND

If anyone worships the beast and its image, and receives a mark on his forehead or on his hand...

— Revelations 14:9

There are three major lines in the hand: the Life line, the Head line and the Heart line (fig. 8.1). Before you begin to read about the different lines, I would like to point out that all the lines, without exception, should be clear and unbroken. When there are marks on the line, the energy of the line is being interfered with. This does not mean that you cannot change the outcome of the lines. You can get rid of certain markings through your change in attitude or through constructive channeling. So, if you do not like what the markings infer, then look at the meaning and find a way to alter the situation. You are in control of your life and of the lines in you hand.

The Life Line

The **Life line**, the line of vitality, shows the physical energy flow. Since it is the combined results of our mental, emotional and physical currents, the Life line will show problems that will have either a mental or emotional basis. If we have allowed the mental or the emotional factors of our makeup to injure or weaken the physical energy flow, the Life line can show death, but there will be many other corroborating signs in the hand to support this reading.

THREE MAJOR LINES

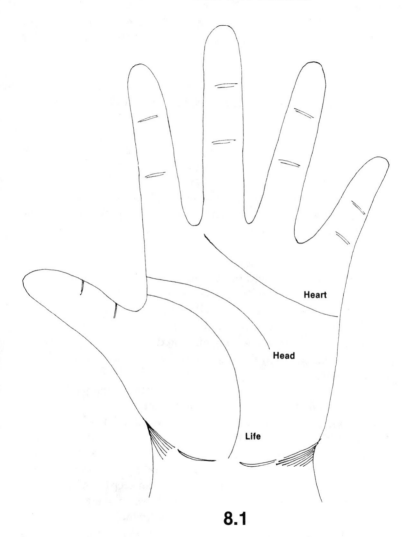

8.1

The Beginning of the Life Life
The Life line usually starts at a midway point between the Jupiter finger and the thumb and then continues in a circular pattern around the Mount of Venus (fig. 8.2).

If the Life line starts above the Head line or on the Mount of Jupiter (fig. 8.3), this would usually show an ambitious, calculating person who would stop at nothing to reach his goals.

If the Life line starts from the thumb (fig. 8.4), the person can be controlled by his emotional attachments, which would include his family. His decisions would tend to be both emotional and impulsive.

The Ending of the Life Line
A short Life line (fig. 8.5) does not by itself indicate death but can show that one has stopped doing things that are purposeful, thus leaving the person feeling unfulfilled.

I once read for a young man who was about thirty years of age. His Life line stopped at approximately thirty-three years of age. I could see no other indications of physical disaster on either his Head or Heart line, but his palm did show an impulsive nature, a person who wants to experience all the sensations of life, including drugs and alcohol. He was already heavily into drugs and, like so many people with his type of psychological makeup, he was also into gambling. About a year later I found out from a close friend of his that he had given up his job, taken all the money he had and gone into the mountains. He was virtually doing nothing but getting high on drugs, sleeping and eating. His physical energy had no directional force. This was indicated by his short Life line.

A Life line that encircles the Mount of Venus, going all the way around the thumb (fig. 8.6), usually shows a person who has inherited a good physical constitution and should live to a ripe old age.

A Life line that ends in a fork (fig. 8.7) can show a diminishing of energy. It is not something to be overly concerned about because as we get into our sixties, seventies and eighties, our energy usually does diminish. Of course, it need not diminish. We can keep ourselves healthy and active lifelong. Naturally, proper diet and exercise are very important in maintaining good health and energy lifelong. A sense of purpose or meaning (through a career, good works, etc.) is also very valuable. Intimate relationships provide necessary emotional support. Keeping a good network of friends, relatives and loved ones is essential. And many people find that faith in something Higher assist them in coping with life.

If the Life line takes a marked direction towards the Luna Mount

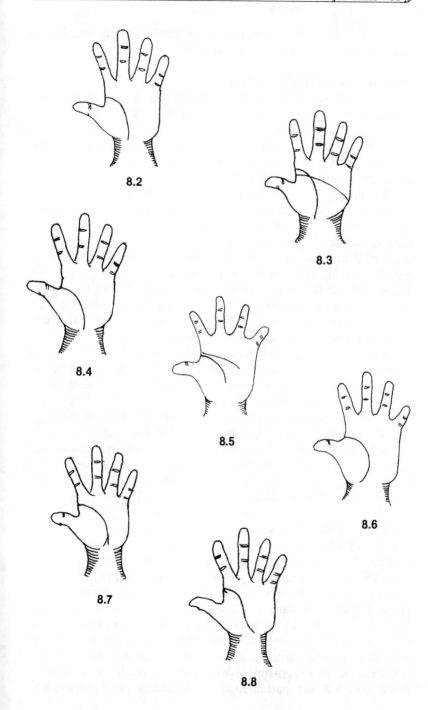

8.2

8.3

8.4

8.5

8.6

8.7

8.8

(fig. 8.8), the individual could have an overactive imagination. If used constructively, this person could be a great fiction writer.

The Arc Around the Venus Mount
If the arc around the Venus Mount is wide (fig. 8.9), the person will generally have a good reservoir of energy and will usually be warm, friendly and an extrovert.

If the arc is narrow (fig. 8.10), the reverse is indicated. The person with this arc will tend to be introverted and may seem cold but, in reality he just enjoys being by himself.

Palmists have known for years that this area of the hand seems to deal with children and procreation. On one side of the palm we have the unconscious, passive zone, which contains the Moon or Luna Mount, the sign in astrology and in ancient teachings of the mother force, of intuition, creativity and birth. On the opposite side of the palm, parallel to Luna, we have the conscious, passive zone, which houses Venus, the planet of love and affection. In palmistry we find family attachments in this area. These two mounts, if equally developed and free of fine cross lines, would indicate an emotional and physical capacity to function in the role of creation or having children.

I have found narrow arcs on men who have had vasectomies and on women who have had their tubes tied before having any children. The narrow arc indicates a choice to the client on procreation. When difficulties in conception are due to a physical problem — such as a tipped uterus, ovarian problems, too-low or too-high sperm counts — then the arc isn't necessarily narrow. The problem may be indicated by the Mount of Venus being very lined and underdeveloped; the Mount of Luna lined and elevated; the Life line tipping abruptly towards the Luna Mount; or the third phalange of the Mercury finger being swollen, as discussed in Chapter Six.

Markings on the Life Line
Islands on the Life line (fig. 8.11) can indicate a break in physical energy or illness. You will have to look at the rest of the palm to determine what has caused the physical problem, if it is from physical or emotional roots. E.g., if the Saturn finger is involved, the person may be inclined to work too hard, and illness becomes the body's way of taking a vacation. Or, illness can be an escape from feeling guilty for the person who feels he is never doing "enough." Where the Jupiter finger is involved, overindulgence (in food, drink) or excessive self-confidence leading to rashness is possible. With any illness, dealing with the emotional roots, utilizing spiritual tools (meditation, prayer, healing touch)

as well as treating physical symptoms is the most likely to effect a lasting cure.

A **chained** Life line (fig. 8.12) at the beginning can show a person who had very delicate health as a child. If the chain continues all the way through, the person may have physical frailty all his life. This is not meant to sound fatalistic. We are responsible for our choices which we are subconsciously aware of. If your client wants health and that is what he has set up for himself, then he will have health. Health is the natural state of the human body. Disease is our choice. The subject can help maintain health through emotional detachment. Detachment can be assisted through yoga, meditation, hypnosis, positive thinking, *tai chi*, etc.

Dots (fig. 8.13) can indicate serious illnesses, especially when the dot becomes discolored, taking on a purple hue.

Crosses on the inside of the Life line, not touching the line (fig. 8.14), as stated earlier, usually show a serious illness to your client. Crosses on the outside of the Life line, touching the line (fig. 8.15), generally show a serious illness or death of someone close to your client. Crosses at the beginning of the Life line (fig. 8.16) suggest a move for your client when very young. I have also seen crosses at the beginning indicating a divorce or separation in the family. A cross touching the inside of the Life line or on the Life line, with the Life line becoming either very wavy afterwards or very light in density (fig. 8.17) may show death. You will have to check the Head or Heart line for further corroborating evidence, such as a dot or island on the corresponding lines at the same time as the cross appears on the Life line.

Breaks in the Life line can show change. The change can be due to many things: a move, a new job, a divorce, etc. If the break is followed by an overlapping line (fig. 8.18), the change will usually be smooth. If, however, the break is sudden and the Life line just picks up and continues without any overlapping (fig. 8.19), the transition will generally be traumatic for your client.

It is important to remember that often **what** happens to us is not as important as **how we feel** about what happens — how we react. People may not always be able to change life events, but they do have control over their own attitudes and reactions. We can choose to react to a change with tension, anxiety, trauma and fear, or we can choose to react with excitement, optimism and pleasure.

A crossbar coming from the inside of the Life line and cutting the line may indicate a specific disease and an operation. The direction of the crossbar after it cuts the Life line will indicate more. If that line goes to the Saturn Mount, the ailment could be with the bones, joints,

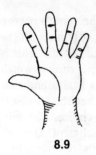

8.9

8.10

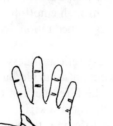

8.11

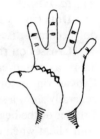

8.12

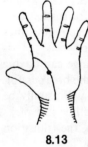

8.13

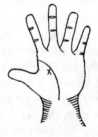

8.14

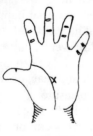

8.15

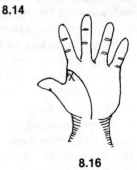

8.16

teeth or ears. If the crossbar ends on the Upper Mount of Mars terminating in a grid, there may be bronchial trouble. If the crossbar terminates at the Heart line, especially if there are corroborating signs of a dot or island, there is a possibility of heart problems. If the crossbar terminates on the lower portion of Luna with a cross or island, female troubles or kidney ailments are a potential.

Remember, that we can help maintain heath by taking care of ourselves physically, remaining open spiritually and dealing with emotional conflicts.

Protections
A **square** touching the Life line (fig. 8.20) can show protection from physical disease or accident. Traditionally, this mark showed imprisonment or the life of a hermit.

A good Mercury line or Mars line will counteract a deficient life line.

Time on the Life Line
There are a number of ways to read time on the Life line, but the one I have found the most useful is the one diagramed by Judith Hipskind (fig. 8.21).

First, establish what is called the thirty-five-year mark. Draw an imaginary line down the middle of the Saturn finger and continue this line until you meet the Life line. This is the thirty-five-year mark. There will usually be one section longer than the other. Whichever section is longer will show the most important portion of life to that individual, whether it will be the first thirty-five years of life or from the age of thirty-five on.

Now, divide the top section into five equal parts. Each section will represent seven years.

Take the second half and divide it into three sections. The first section will represent the years 36 - 50, the second section will represent the years 50 - 70 and the last section will represent the years beyond age 70.

Test Yourself #8.a

1. A Life line shows what? _____
2. Where is the usual starting place for the Life line? _____
3. If the Life line starts from the thumb, what might be indicated?
_____

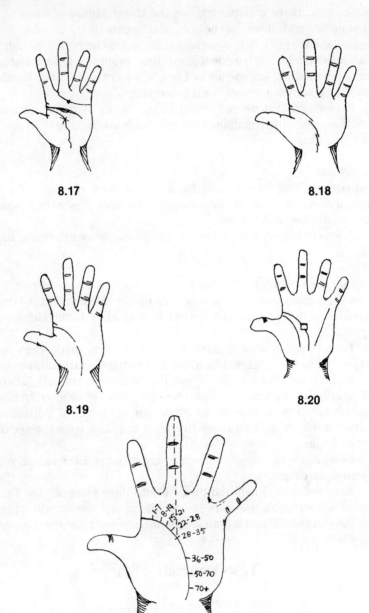

8.17

8.18

8.19

8.20

8.21

4. If the Life line starts above the Head line or the Mount of Jupiter, it suggests what? _____

5. What does a short Life line imply? _____

6. The arc around the Venus Mount shows what? _____

7. Dots on the Life line can indicate _____ .

8. A crossbar that cuts the Life line and goes to the Saturn Mount implies ailments with the _____,
_____, or _____ .
What can the person do to help themselves get better and/or stay well? _____

9. A crossbar that terminates at the Heart line, especially if there is corroborating evidence of an island or dot, suggests _____ problems.
What are some options for maintaining health in this area?
_____

10. A crossbar going to the Upper Mount of Mars, terminating in a grid could show _____.

11. What two lines will counterbalance the implications of a weak Life line? _____ and _____ .

12. Explain the difference between influence lines and Mars lines.
_____

The Head Line

The **Head line** reveals the scope of mental interests, imagination and mental independence.

The Beginning of the Head Line

The Head line usually begins between the thumb and the Jupiter finger and is often connected to the line of life (fig. 8.22), but the Head line can start inside the Life line or be separated from it.

If the Head line is connected to the Life line at the beginning, we usually find a cautious person, one who thinks before he acts. If, however, that Head line remains connected to the Life line for a long distance, we find a person who may feel inferior, a person who held on to the apron strings too long. This person usually does not "find himself" until later in life.

The Head line that begins from the inside of the Life line (fig. 8.23) generally indicates a person who feels a need for protection and because of this he will be defensive about his sensitivities. He may not want to see the world or the truth for fear of being hurt. He might not trust anyone but himself and, sadly enough, he often does not trust himself.

If the Head line is separated from the Life line (fig. 8.24), we have a more independent person, one who is not afraid to try things or to fall on his face. The only problem here is that this person may prove to be too impulsive and get himself into hot water. On the positive side, the separated Life and Head lines show an intuitive streak. This person evaluates situations and other people instantly and is usually correct in his evaluation.

The End of the Head Line
The termination of the Head line will indicate the mental expression of your client. If the Head line travels straight across the palm to the percussion side of the hand (fig. 8.25), the person will have an analytical, mathematical mind. This person will have a practical outlook about everything but can be so practical and so sure of his own judgment that he suffers from an acute case of tunnel vision.

The curved line, one that travels to the Mount of Lune (fig. 8.26), shows a creative, intuitive streak that would prove beneficial for the poet, the writer and the artist. If, however, the curve into Luna is really sharp and deep into the mount (fig. 8.27), we may find emotional and mental instability. This person could live in his imagination and be totally unconventional. If there are other saving graces in the hand (a good strong thumb, developed knuckles or a long Jupiter finger), the person has the strength to combat the stimuli from the fantasy world. Otherwise, the person might live completely in the clouds and be mentally unbalanced, even suicidal.

The Head line sometimes ends in a fork (fig. 8.28). The fork shows that your client can see two sides of an issue. The directions of the prongs will show the diversity of interest. If one prong were to go to Luna and one prong to Upper Mars (fig. 8.29), we have the markings of the artistic soul who also has practical, common sense. This person will find an outlet where both the practical and the artistic natures can converge into one, such as an architect. The prong that is the longest will determine the strongest inclination. If, however, the prongs were to divide with one going to Upper Mars and the other going towards Mercury (fig. 8.30), we find the professional business person, the lawyer, the politician.

Marking on the Head Line
Islands on the Head line (fig. 8.31) are serious and can show head injuries, mental disorders. Any time you have such a severity of disease, the markings will also be confirmed by markings on either the Heart line or the Life line, or both. You will have to note the approximate

8.22

8.23

8.24

8.25

8.26

8.27

time when the strain may happen and caution your client to avoid tax-
ing himself at that time. Your client always has the choice to change
the situation coming up in the future. Sometimes all this takes is a
change in attitude.

Chains on the Head line can show bad concentration and
confusion.

Dots on the Head line, especially if under the Saturn finger, may
indicate eye strain.

Breaks in the Head line show headaches and lack of concentration. If the line of head shows a complete, unmended break beneath
the Mount of Saturn, there is the possibility of sudden death or
misadventure. As always, you will have to check your other major lines
to confirm and determine the possible cause.

Severely broken Head lines show a possibility of mental imbalance.
This is especially true when the Mount of Luna is overdeveloped, showing an overactive imagination, and when either the Mercury finger or
the thumb is short, or the shape of the fingers is distorted (fig. 8.32).

Studies performed with the mentally retarded or maladjusted patients show that the majority of them have breaks on the Head line
or unusually short Head lines (fig. 8.33)[8].

Time on the Head Line
I read the time on the Head line in the same way I gauge the time on
the Life line. Some palmists use the fingers and spaces between the
fingers as measuring points, giving ten years to each mark. I have found
the former method (pp. 85-86) much more accurate.

Test Yourself #8.b

1. List three different starting places for the Head line.
   A. _____
   B. _____
   C. _____
2. Of these three, which could show an independent, compulsive
   nature? _____
3. Which could indicate a defensive person? _____
4. Which could indicate a cautious person? _____
5. List three adjectives that might explain the person with the Head
   line that travels straight across the palm ending on the percussion.
   _____
6. What does a fork at the end of the Head line suggest?
   _____

---

8. Wolff, Charlotte. *The Hand in Psychological Diagnosis*. London, England:
1951.

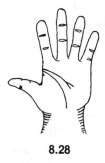

8.28

8.29

8.30

8.31

8.32

8.33

7. If the Head line were to travel sharply into the Mount of Luna, what advice would you have for your client? _____

The Heart Line

The **Heart line** is a gauge for emotional sensitivities and indicates the health or disease of the heart organ.

The Beginnings of the Heart Line
There are disputes among palmists as to the beginning of this line. Some maintain that it starts under the Mercury finger while others believe that it starts under the Jupiter finger. I feel this line's natural starting place is under the Mercury finger since this finger deals with our most intimate relationships and with communication on all levels. Emotions are a subjective, unconscious energy form, and it would make sense that the Heart line, which is the channel for our emotional personality, would travel from the unconscious part of our hand to the conscious part, to the Jupiter Mount.

The Length of the Heart Line
The length of the Heart line varies like all the major lines. If this line travels all the way across the palm, ending in a curve (fig. 8.34), we usually find a warm personality, human and understanding sometimes to the point of putting his loved ones on a pedestal and seeing only their good side.

A Heart line of normal length ends between the Jupiter and Saturn fingers (fig. 8.35), showing the person to be balanced in his emotional feelings: warm, yet practical.

The short Heart line, or the one that ends under Saturn (fig. 8.36), tends to show the person who thinks of himself before anyone else. In this case, the unconscious, emotional self never breaks into the active, conscious area of the hand so that expressing love and concern for others is very difficult. This is a selfish line, but I have found that the person with the short Heart line often has tried his hardest to understand and to work with relationships. He is usually very frustrated because he does not understand the whole emotional facet of his being. You could suggest to your client that he get involved in areas or careers that deal with service to others such as rehabilitation programs, helping the elderly, etc. This will help your client deal with and understand his emotional capacities.

A good example of this is a lady that I read for at a small social gathering a few years ago. Her Heart line stopped short of Saturn. She had been married very early and the marriage did not work out, ending in divorce. She was so upset with her own "failing" as a wife that she ended up in the hospital with anorexia, a disease where the person stops eating, subconsciously starving herself for punishment. She had to be fed intravenously and did survive. She has since been married and divorced, gone through numerous relationships, and is still searching for the answer behind the word **love**.

The Course of the Heart Line
The course of the Heart line indicates how the person shows his emotions. If the Heart line is straight, crossing the palm (fig. 8.37), you generally have an independent person who may be cold and who might not want close relationships because it would take away his independence. This person may not express his feelings no matter how deeply he may feel them. He will want to be in control emotionally.

If the line travels in a sweep ending between the Jupiter and Saturn finger (fig. 8.38), the person has a healthy attitude toward others and is someone who will express his feelings.

If the Heart line swings towards the Head line, the traditional meaning was that the subject may have asexual or homosexual tendencies whether practiced or not.

As someone pointed out to me, the definitions of asexual and homosexual are quite different, so how can this one line define both practices? That is a valid question.

What I have found in studying the course of the Heart line was that a line that swings towards the Head line often indicates repressed sexual energy due to fear or apprehension. The swing can also indicate that the Heart line, or emotions, is ruled by the Head line, or the mind.

The Heart line that terminates in a fork (fig. 8.39) shows a strong desire for expression which could indicate a flirtatious disposition.

Markings on the Heart Line
An **island** on the Heart line can shows weakness in the heart. This weakness can be brought on by emotional trauma and disappointments, by taking things too seriously (too much "to heart").

A **chained** Heart line (fig. 8.40) shows a volatile person who may wish to learn to control his emotions. Of course, such people may enjoy the excitement of an intensely emotional life and thrive on the ups and downs it entails.

Dots on the Heart line (fig. 8.41) show a shock to the individual which can happen from the loss of a loved one. If the dot is discolored and under the Mercury or Uranus finger, this dot can indicate sexual

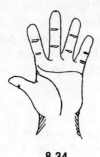

8.34

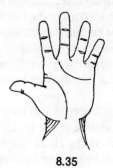

8.35

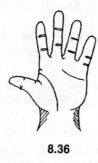

8.36

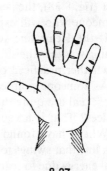

8.37

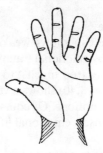

8.38

harassment. The person needs to get in touch with his own sexuality and make use of his sexual energies. Dots can disappear if situation is handled constructively. No one has to be a victim.

A **cross** on the Heart line shows emotional loss, or the death of a loved one. You can verify this by checking the Life line for the loss of a loved one.

A **square** touching the Heart line (fig. 8.42) shows protection from emotional trauma. This protection could come from another person, guardian or parent — someone who helps you through an emotional time, making it easier to handle.

A **crossbar** that cuts the Life line and terminates in a break, dot or island on the Heart line under the finger of Uranus (fig. 8.43), can show heart problems.

Heart disease is the largest cause of death in the world. Much of this is related to stress due to constant pressure and a compulsive need to do everything just right and as fast as we can. Through relaxation techniques, biofeedback and hypnosis, we can control and reduce trauma to the heart. Diet and exercise can also be extremely effective in strengthening the cardiovascular system.

The Simian Line
Sometimes the Heart line will run into the Head line and form a single traverse line which runs across the hand, forming what is called a **simian line** (fig. 8.44). This line, when present, usually represents inner tension because there is the combining of the Head line, which starts in the conscious zone, and the Heart line, which starts in the unconscious zone. The person is usually at odds between his mind and his heart.

Only about three to five percent of the population have a simian line. It is considered an atavistic sign and medically shows up in congenital abnormalities such as mongolism and in people who suffer from leukemia. On the positive side, this line can show intense concentration and ambition to carry out desired goals.

Fred Gettings found that this line is also present with very religious and artistic people. The clue to the way a person will use the inner tension indicated by this line will show in the rest of his hand. If there are negative signs, such as a twisted or small Mercury finger, a short thumb, or the person has all arch patterns on the fingers, the chances are that he may release the inner tension in a destructive way. If the hand has positive traits, the person will probably elevate the tension to either creation or spirituality.

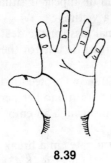

8.39

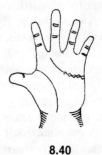

8.40

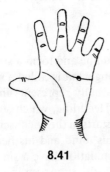

8.41

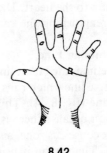

8.42

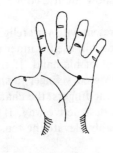

8.43

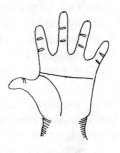

8.44

Received under automatic writing:

Question: I would like to ask you about the simian line. What are the karmic implications involved with the combined line?

Answer: A lot of it has to do with pain: the pain of hating, the pain of not allowing others to live. The Heart line is virtually taken away from the person and given to the Head line, to the mind. It was used poorly last time so it is given up to the mental side of the personality. Simian people feel like caged animals with their emotions. Their emotions are dealt with in a structured manner, which is frustrating. Until they learn how to calm themselves and how to accept the prison, they are caught. Once they learn that their prison is their own feelings and attitudes, the line is not binding anymore. A lot of them have hated so intensely that they had to come back to learn what it is like to want to feel, yet be inhibited in their emotional expression.

In the case of Mongoloid children, they are allowing someone else to love them, love them totally. They are sweet and docile. They have come to play the opposite end of the spectrum by allowing themselves to be loved and cared for. They are not caught anymore in the cage but are oblivious to the prison.

One person has the pain of not knowing how to express his feelings and wanting to, and the other person, the mongoloid, is allowing others to completely feel.

Match Them Up #8.c

1. Very warm personality that will only see the best ____
2. Looking for emotional fulfillment ____
3. Independent, cold person ____
4. Possibly asexual or homosexual ____
5. Balanced, healthy attitude toward others ____
6. Head and Heart line combined ____
7. A flirt ____
8. Emotional trauma ____

A . Simian line

B . Forked ending

C . Island on the Heart line

D . Goes all the way across the palm, ending in a curve

E . Line goes all the way across the palm

F . Short Heart line

G . Travels toward the head line

H . Ends between the Jupiter and Saturn fingers.

CHAPTER NINE

THE MINOR LINES OF THE HAND

The Fate Line

The **fate line** is also known as the Saturn Line, the Career Line or the Line of Destiny. This line appears most often on the conic, psychic, or philosophical hand and rarely on the square or spatulate hand.

This line shows an inner adaptability to the changes in this world and a strong sense of purpose. However, this line does not by itself indicate success in life or recognition. One must depend on the context of the rest of the hand to determine if success will be achieved. Other indications could include a strong thumb, a clear Life line or Head line showing that the person has good physical and/or mental energies to carry out goals.

The Start of the Fate Lines

Palmists do not agree about the beginning of the fate line. Some say it starts under the Saturn finger and runs towards the wrist. Others claim it starts at the bottom of the hand and travels towards the fingers. I start from the wrist and go towards the fingers or active region of the hand.

If the fate line begins at the center of the palm and travels towards the Saturn finger (fig. 9.1), the person is likely to be self-sufficient and have a balanced outlook on life. After all, the Saturn finger is the divider: the balance between the conscious and the unconscious areas of the palm.

If the fate line begins from the Venus Mount or from the life line and travels upwards (fig. 9.2), the person's success or goals in life are often through family connections. This can also show family or home restrictions at an early age — maybe someone who had to go out and support a family.

If the fate line starts from the Luna Mount (fig. 9.3), the success may be dependent upon others. This can show a public career or work dealing with the public. Being in the limelight helps make this person successful.

The fate line beginning from either the Venus Mount or from the Luna Mount shows a dependency on others to succeed. Due to that dependency, the people can be too sensitive to the criticism of others, not have enough faith in themselves or lack the ability to stand on their own two feet.

Sometimes there exists a double fate line which will generally indicate more than one career. This line can be mistaken for a companion line, or sister line, to the fate line. The way to tell the double fate line and the companion line apart will be through the density of the line. The companion line will be lighter in density than the double fate line (fig. 9.4).

A companion line shows a close personal relationship or affection. This can show a marriage, but you will have to confirm this by looking at the union lines and checking the times on both lines (see p. 101). By marriage I am referring to a relationship and that does not necessarily mean a marital contract. The companion line can also show a person who will help your client achieve her goals.

The Ending of the Fate Lines
The fate line usually ends on the Saturn Mount but can end on any of the finger mounts, making many of the lines confusing to both the beginner and the expert.

If the fate line were to travel to the Jupiter Mount (fig. 9.5), the ability to lead and to advise others is shown.

If the fate line travels to the Uranus Mount (fig. 9.6), this shows the possibility of a creative or artistic career.

If the line travels towards the Mercury Mount (fig. 9.7), it shows a potential for business or scientific career, or writing.

A Saturn line that ends with a trident on the Mount of Saturn (fig. 9.8) shows the person is likely to have personal recognition.

Sometimes the fate line ends before reaching one of the finger mounts. If the fate line were to end at the Head line (fig. 9.9), the person's goals were either achieved by the age of thirty-five or the goals were stopped or interfered with. Check to see if an interference line crosses the Life line at the same time.

If the fate line ends at the Heart line (fig. 9.10), the goals were achieved by the time the person was fifty years old. If the fate line ends

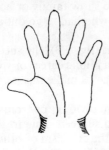

9.1

9.2

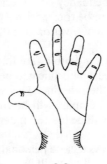

9.3

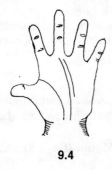

9.4

9.5

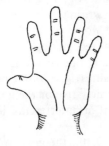

9.6

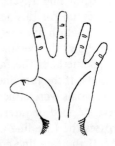

9.7

at the Heart line with either a dot or an island on the Heart line itself, this could indicate that the career was ended due to heart troubles or death. Check for crosses or islands on the Life line at the same time.

A fate line that starts at the Heart line and travels to the Saturn finger (fig. 9.11) shows that the person finds purposes late in life, after she has reached the age of fifty.

As stated before, the fate line by itself does not guarantee success or recognition, and sometimes you will find a very successful person with no fate line at all. In this case, the person will have other strong markings: a good Uranus line; a good, strong thumb and index fingers; whorls on her fingers; or a good Mercury line.

Markings on the Fate Line
Islands on the Saturn line show financial troubles or losses, which will last the length of the island (fig. 9.12).

A **chained** fate line shows uncertainty and vacillation in the world.

A **crossbar** cutting the Saturn line shows obstacles to success due to illness, or to the interference of others in the person's life.

Breaks (fig. 9.13) show impediments to the career but can also show a new direction in a career or a location change.

Age on the Fate Line
Age on the fate line is read from the wrist to the fingers (fig. 9.14). At the point where the fate line crosses the Head line is considered approximately thirty-five years of age. The point where the fate line crosses the Heart line is approximately fifty years of age.

Divide the section from the wrist to the Head line into five sections, each section representing seven years. The section between the head and the Heart lines, or the **quadrangle**, is a period of fifteen years. The area between the Heart line and the fingers is from fifty years on. There are times when the Head line or the Heart line is below or above the normal position, and in this case you will have to adjust the time sequence accordingly.

Test Yourself #9.a

1. What does the fate line show? _____
2. Does the fate line by itself indicate success in life? _____
3. Where would the fate line begin that would suggest early family or home restrictions? _____
4. How do you tell a companion line from a double fate line, and what does a companion line indicate? _____
5. How do you tell age on the fate line? _____

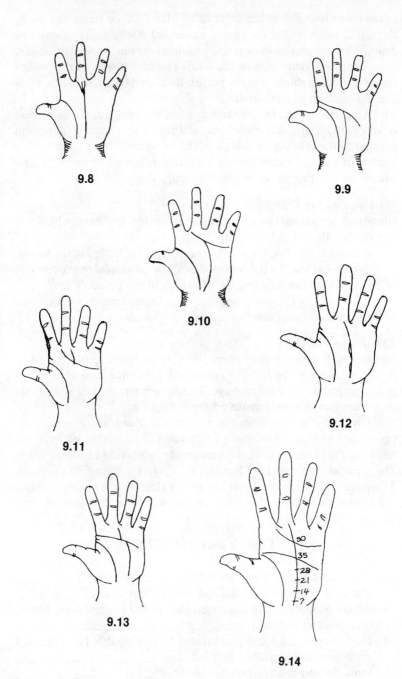

9.8

9.9

9.10

9.11

9.12

9.13

9.14

The Sun Line

The **Sun line** is also known as the Apollo Line, the Line of Brilliancy and the Line of Luck and Fame. The line indicates talent. The direction of that talent will depend on the rest of the hand. Whenever this line is present, it shows that the person has the ability to make friends, money and a reputation.

The Start of the Sun Line
The Sun line also travels from the wrist to the Uranus finger and, like the fate line, will show what spurs the talent on; for self-confidence, the line begins in the center of the palm. The talent shown through inherited qualities starts at the Life line. For public recognition, the Sun line will begin at the Mount of Luna.

Sometimes you will see a Sun line that starts from the Mount of Upper Mars (fig. 9.15). This shows the ability to fight for fame and recognition.

When the Sun line begins from either the Head or the Heart line (fig. 9.16), the talents will often be achieved later in life.

The Ending of the Sun Line
The Sun line ends on the Uranus Mount under the Uranus finger.

Markings on the Sun Line
Islands on the Sun line (fig. 9.17) show a loss of reputation, a dangerous intrigue that can bring disaster into the person's life.

Bars show impediments to success. If the Sun line ends abruptly after the bar crosses it (fig. 9.18), the career has been ended because of health problems.

A **star** at the end of the Sun line on the Uranus Mount (fig. 9.19) indicates success in the arts as a writer, musician, painter or showman.

The Mercury Line

The **Mercury line** is also called the Line of Health, the Line of Liver and the Line of Intuition.

The Mercury line, depending on where it starts, will show business acumen, health (especially of the digestive organs) and intuitive faculties. Whenever you find this line present, you will find someone who has an inner sensitivity to her own physical body, physically or spiritually; it is emphasized as inner knowing.

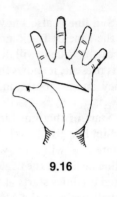

9.16

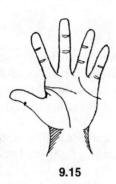

9.15

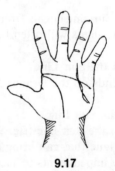

9.17

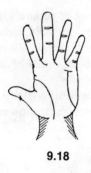

9.18

9.19

The Start of the Mercury Line

The Mercury line that starts in the lower part of the hand, near the Life line, and travels in a straight, slanted line towards the Mercury Mount (fig. 9.20) shows success in business, and good vitality and health.

In the old school of palmistry, if the Mercury line joined with the Life line at any point, that point was supposed to indicate the time death would occur. I have not been able to verify this. I feel that we need to do many more studies before we can establish with any degree of certainty that a connection of the Life line with the Mercury line means death.

When the Mercury line starts from the Mount of Luna and travels in a semicircle ending on the upper Mount of Mars or the Mount of Mercury (fig. 9.21), the person has what is commonly referred to as a Line of Intuition. This indicates psychic powers.

The Ending of the Mercury Line

The Mercury line ends on the Mercury Mount or sometimes on Upper Mars.

Markings on the Mercury Line

A Mercury line that has **islands** on most or all of its length can show throat and respiratory infections.

Sensitivity of the stomach and digestive system are indicated by **loops** on the Mercury line.

A **delicate line** shows delicate health.

A **broken arch** shows that psychic abilities are turned on and off; the energy is not allowed to flow.

Test Yourself #9.b

1. Four other names for the Sun line are:

   _____

   _____

   _____

   _____

2. The Sun line indicates _____

3. The ability to fight for fame and recognition will be seen in the Sun line that starts from _____

4. The Sun line ends on the _____

5. A bar on the Sun line, when the line ends abruptly might indicate

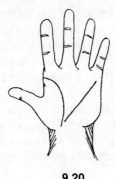

9.20

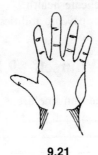

9.21

6. A star or triangle at the end of the Sun line on the Uranus Mount shows _____ in the _____
7. Three other names for the Mercury line are _____
_____
8. A Mercury line that starts from the Mount of Luna and travels in a semicircle ending on Upper Mars or the Mount of Mercury represents _____ abilities.
9. Loops on the Mercury line could suggest diseases of the _____ and digestive system.
10. Throat and respiratory infections are implied by a Mercury line that is _____ the majority of the way.
What are some of the alternatives an individual can follow to achieve health in this area? _____

Union Lines

Am I going to get married? Will I have another relationship? These are the most frequently asked questions from clients. To find the answer, look at the **union lines**.

The union lines are also referred to as marriage lines. They are found on the Mercury Mount under the Mercury finger in the space between the Heart line and the starting of the Mercury finger (fig. 9.22).

To refer to these lines as marriage lines is misleading because the institution of marriage was created by man and a marital contract does not have to exist to constitute a union. If your client asks you if she is going to get married or remarried, you will have to explain just what the union lines mean.

Another interesting factor about the union lines is that the relationship does not have to be a sexual relationship to show up in this area. I have seen union lines on people who are carrying on a liaison that is based on love, understanding and friendship, divorced from the sexual act due to their philosophical or religious views. It is still a union, and if seen in this area of the hand, shows a strong impact on your client.

The union line, if straight, clear and unbroken (fig. 9.23), speaks of a strong connection where the two people will stay and work together in harmony and towards a constructive end.

When the line has a sister line next to it, making it look like two parallel lines (fig. 9.24), the relationship, though rocky at times, will stay together due to the added protection and strength symbolized by the sister line.

When the union line is forked at the end (fig. 9.25), this shows separation. It does not necessarily have to mean divorce or separation as we think of it. Today, the family unit has changed. This has happened for many reasons: more opportunities for travel, education, and jobs for both the male and the female. Many couples who are married are acting independently of each other and still maintaining their union. The fork does indicate freedom for the two individuals. How the separation is conducted will depend on the sensitivity and security or insecurity of the couple involved.

If one of the prongs of the fork is crossed by a crossbar (fig. 9.26) and there is confirmation of death of a loved one on the Life line, the separation on the union line could be from the death of the partner.

Markings on the Union Line
If the union line has an **island** (fig. 9.27), there may be domestic trouble. This could be due to money problems (check the fate line for islands or breaks), infidelity (check the Sun line for islands), or just personal changes and growth away from the partner.

If the union line has a square (fig. 9.28), the marital problems will be solved or the union will be protected by the inner strength of the two people involved.

Age on the Union Line
I have found timing in this section of the palm to be inaccurate. I am still trying to find a clue to a more precise answer. Traditionally you are told to find the center of this area. On a woman's hand, for some reason, this mark will stand for about twenty-five years of age. Any union line closer to the Heart line shows a younger union, and usually a more emotional one. Any line closer to the Mercury finger shows an older union and usually more of a mental, objective type (fig. 9.29).

On a man's hand, however, the center point represents thirty years of age. As I have already stated, I don't find this an accurate record so please do not use this as an infallible bit of information.

Density
The stronger the line, the stronger the emotional and mental attachment. This does not necessarily mean a happy union. Pain and suffering also have emotional and mental factors.

A very light line shows that the attachment was not as emotional as the person might think. Of course, when the person is involved, it is not always easy to tell her that the relationship is not that emotional.

If this area of the hand has no union lines, this usually shows a person who is not concerned with one-on-one relationships. Personal attachments are not a major priority.

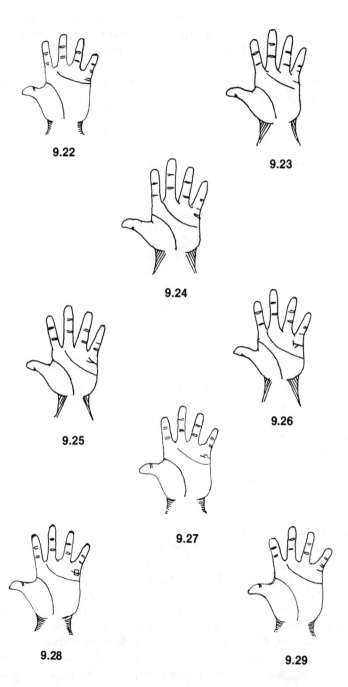

9.22

9.23

9.24

9.25

9.26

9.27

9.28

9.29

Sometimes you will even find that a marriage will not register on the hand. For example, I read for a young man who had come to this country from Italy. He told me that he wanted to make a success for himself and that he had married his first wife for financial reasons and really had not cared for her at all. There was no union line on this man's hand until later in life.

Test Yourself #9.c

1. The Union lines are also referred to as the _____ lines.
2. The Union lines are found on the _____ mount under the _____ finger.
3. Separation can show by the Union line _____ at the end.
4. Death of a spouse might show by a _____ Union line with a _____ cutting through one of the prongs.
5. Domestic troubles could be suggested if there is an _____ on the Union line.
6. The middle point in this area is read as _____ years for women and _____ years for men.

The Children Lines

In most spheres of palmistry, the **children lines** are located under the Mercury finger on the percussion and are recognized as perpendicular lines to the union lines (fig. 9.30.1).

Logically, this seems a valid place for these lines since the Mercury finger does deal with our most intimate relationships, and deviations in this finger can show problems with the opposite sex and with the reproductive organs. However, due to the many lines found in this vicinity, I decided to look for another area that would prove more accurate for reading the lines of children.

During my course of study I came across a book written by Myrah Lawrance called *Hand Analysis* in which she postulates about the children line being located in the wrist area, under the health bracelet rather than under the Mercury finger (fig. 9.30.2). The majority of palmists consider this area an indicator of physical energy and longevity, each line supposedly representing twenty-six to thirty years of life. Thus, if one were to possess three such lines, one would live to around ninety years of age. Saint Germain, who was an early advocate of this theory, stated that if the first bracelet on the wrist were high and convex in form, there would be problems in childbearing and in the reproductive systems, so the Lawrance theory bore some consideration. The best backing, however, for Lawrance's theory came from the readings of women's hands. In the course of investigation I found that the lines under the health bracelet not only told the number of children one might have, but also would indicate twins, miscarriages and abortions.

A clear, unbroken line under the health bracelet, crossing two-thirds of the distance of the wrist, indicates a living child. If the line ends less than halfway across the wrist, then the child has probably died in early infancy.

If a line travels up towards the health bracelet, is badly islanded, broken or not complete (fig. 9.30.3), the conception may have miscarried or aborted.

Abortions can also be shown by a deep dot on one of these lines (fig. 9.30.7). One woman whose hands I read had a dot so deep it was purple, disfiguring this area of her wrist. This area of her wrist actually looked as though it had a double chin. The woman, only in her early thirties, had had four abortions (fig. 9.30.7).

If the line travels the width of the wrist but is islanded or becomes lighter in density (fig. 9.30.4), there is a possibility of the child having poor health.

Twins are shown by a double parallel line (fig. 9.30.5). These lines ride so close to each other that they sometimes touch.

Twins are also shown by a single line that ends in a fork (fig. 9.30.6).

There is further speculation that the sex of the child can be determined by the density of the lines: the darker line being the male and the lighter line being the female. The only problem here is that if there is only one line, there is nothing to compare the density of the line with and, as I have mentioned before, the light density can indicate weak health in the child and is not necessarily an indication of gender. Furthermore, when dealing in the metaphysical world, sex is not an absolute; the light line can show a masculine gender but a person who is very sensitive, artistic, creative and vice versa.

The number of children does not always show on only one wrist but can be found as a composite of lines on both wrists. I read for a woman who had six children; three showed on her right wrist and three showed on her left wrist.

Remember that the children lines, like the union line, do not necessarily show only one's biological children, but can show a child that has or will become very close to your client: nephew, niece,

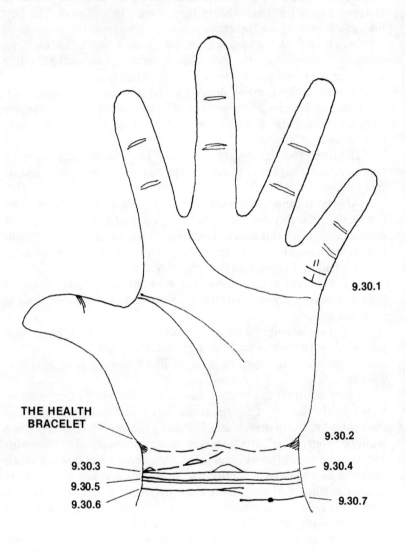

9.30.1

THE HEALTH BRACELET

9.30.2

9.30.3

9.30.4

9.30.5

9.30.6

9.30.7

stepchild or adopted child.

Match them Up #9.d

1. Double parallel line____
2. Dot on children line____
3. Line becomes lighter in density____
4. Line not complete and islanded____
5. A clear, unbroken line____

A. Living child
B. Miscarriage
C. Twins
D. Abortion
E. Child with poor health

The Girdle of Venus

Technically, this is the line that encircles the fingers of Saturn and Uranus, starting between the Jupiter and Saturn fingers and usually ending between the Saturn and Uranus fingers, though at times the line may end on the Mount of Mercury (fig. 9.31).

This line is usually found on the conic or psychic hand, showing up rarely on the square or spatulate hand.

Palmists either disagree on the interpretation of this line or seem to parrot the teachings of the traditional palmists, but there are certain adjectives that keep popping up when you read about it: sensual, sensitive, nervous, intuitive or artistic genius.

According to Saint Germain, if you possess a normal Girdle of Venus, one that encircles the Saturn and Uranus fingers without any markings or breaks, you are artistic and literate. But if the Girdle of Venus is broken or if you have a doubled Girdle of Venus, you will give in to unusual vices as an adult.

Let us look at this line logically. It encompasses the finger and Mount of Saturn (Father Time, the finger of duty, responsibility and deep study) and travels around the finger and Mount of Uranus (the finger in folklore used for healing, the finger of creativity or its counterpart, destruction). What the Girdle of Venus does is bridge the gap between the conscious and the unconscious since the Saturn finger is the divider of these two worlds, bringing together the wisdom and studious nature of Saturn and the power of creation of Uranus.

Let us go back to the adjectives we found ascribed to the Girdle of Venus. These very same adjectives are used in explaining the movement of the life force, which has been called the opening of the serpent or the rising of the *Kundalini*. Traditionally this energy exists at the root chakra, which is located at the base of the spine.

The root chakra is one of the spiritual centers of the body. This chakra, when opened, is a vital and strong force. When it is opened naturally or with appropriate training, it can be the passage to enlightenment, but opened when one is unprepared could lead to extremes in sensuality, insanity or even death. As C. W. Leadbeater says in his book *The Chakras* —

> One very common effect of rousing it prematurely is that it rushes downwards in the body instead of upwards, and thus excites the most undesirable passions, excites them and intensifies their effects to such a degree that it becomes impossible for the man to resist them, because a force has been brought into play in whose presence he is as helpless as a swimmer before the jaws of a shark.[9]

There are seven such spiritual centers of the body, and I postulate that if one has a Girdle of Venus, broken or otherwise, one has come to work on the opening of the fourth chakra, the heart chakra. After all, the Girdle of Venus is often referred to as a sister line to the Heart line. This line has to deal with emotions, relationships and love, and this is why the line, when present, is often considered a sign of sensuality.

There is another interesting fact that comes to light if the Girdle of Venus is looked at as an indication of enlightenment of this spiritual center. When the root chakra is open and flows upwards in its natural course, there seems to be, according to C. W. Leadbeater, a mingling of the two polar forces of the universe, the yin and the yang, the feminine and masculine, until the two unite to become one. Is it not possible that in the course of the opening up of the root chakra, and thus the other spiritual centers of the body, a combining of the sexual bodies are brought into play and that is why the adjectives sensual, sensitive and intuitive are used over and over again in the old palmistry books?

The Girdle of Venus, when complete, unbroken and free of bars or minor lines, shows the potential for great work either in the artistic, literary, religious or political arena.

A break in the Girdle of Venus (fig. 9.32) might show that the intuitive, artistic flow can be broken, causing the person to be irritable, emotional and nervous. This would also explain the so-called "artistic temperament."

An island on the Girdle of Venus (fig. 9.33), especially when the line ends after the island, would show a possibility of emotional or

---

9. Leadbeater, C.W. *The Chakras*, 81-82. Illinois: The Theosophical Publishing House, 1927.

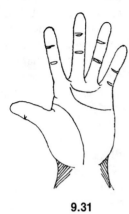

9.31

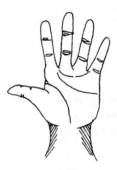

9.32

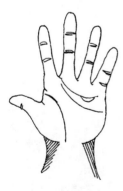

9.33

mental imbalance since the Girdle of Venus is located in the emotional and intuitive part of the palm.

You will have to check the Head line to confirm the same. If this mark happens on the minor hand, and the major hand has a clear Girdle of Venus, the person has begun to use her artistic, intuitive nature instead. Hopefully, this will be what you find rather than an island on the Girdle of Venus and the line stopping on the major hand.

I believe that this line is an indicator of great potential. Sometimes, as in the case of the broken Girdle of Venus, the person will have to work hard to get beyond the nervous and overly sensitive nature, but the potential is there.

Test Yourself #9.e

1. The Girdle of Venus starts _____ and ends
_____ ?

2. What hand type is this line usually found on? _____
   and _____ hands.

3. List four adjectives associated with this line:

   _____   _____

   _____   _____

4. When the Girdle of Venus is stopped by an island, what might be indicated? _____ or _____
   imbalance.

CHAPTER TEN

COMPATIBILITY

The major questions I come across in counseling concern relationships, so I have included a chapter on compatibility.

We bind together with another person who is another facet of ourselves to become more of a whole. So what is the problem? The problem is simply one of growth or stagnation. If people grow through a relationship, the growth itself can cause separation, especially if the partner has not grown at the same time or in the same direction.

Many of us stay together because of children, financial assets, or because the situation is too easy and comfortable, even though we are not happy. Most people have at one time or another told their parents to let go so they could grow. Maybe we should learn to follow our own advice.

Sexual attraction is easy. Growth comes from the struggle, and, hopefully, as the struggle progresses, you will have grown in the same direction as your partner. Otherwise you will have to let go. The following are two examples of married couples who have been together for at least ten years. Did they struggle? You'd better believe it. They have just been lucky enough to change and grow together.

Before we start to examine the hands, it is important that you realize that for compatibility the hands need both differences and similarities. For example, two earth hands might indicate much stagnation or two fire hands might prove too combustible together.

Couple A

They have been together over thirty years.

The man has a spatulate or air hand, the palm is long and square, and the fingers long (fig. 10.1). This shows an intelligent, inquisitive mind, a person who is always getting into new things. He needs the freedom to be able to experience new people and new situations and might find it difficult to be faithful to his wife.

His wife has a square hand (fig. 10.2). She is a practical and conservative person. She would be more of the plodder while he would be the one to initiate the action. She needs the catalyst. She would be loyal to him even though she might entertain ideas of experimentation (she has a Girdle of Venus in her hand). She is also intuitive and creative (the Girdle).

Both of them are right-handed and, as you can see, the angles of the thumbs are open and receptive to others, so social events are welcomed by both.

They both have good spacing between their Uranus and Mercury fingers and their Head and Life lines are separated, showing their independent natures. They are both strong, and they allow each other the space to do their own thing, which is imperative to them.

She has many more fine, web lines in her palm showing her nervousness, while his palm is clearer. They can put up and keep up with each other, although they could also drive each other crazy at times.

Their fate lines show a lot of changes (both in locations and jobs) that a weaker or more sensitive hand could not handle. They would probably go through some good arguments because they are both strong, stubborn and independent.

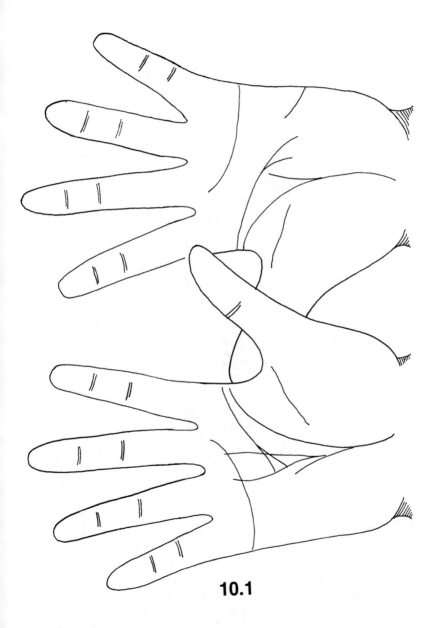

10.1

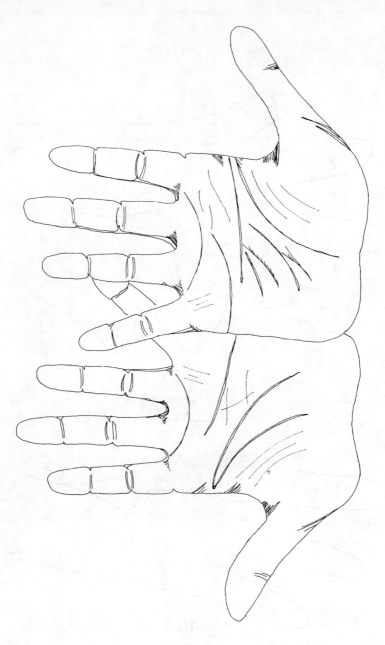

10.2

Couple B

They have been together over twelve years.

Here we have the male with the spatulate hand (fig. 10.4) and the female with the conic or fire hand (fig. 10.3). The male is more down to earth than the female in this instance. The female would show more of an intuitive, emotional approach to everything.

From the shape we know that he likes to organize things while she dislikes details and would rather have fun or be doing something creative. She cannot be bothered with minutia. This difference makes her exciting to him because he cannot totally let go and lie back. She is, in fact, doing this for him.

Both of them have a long Mercury finger which indicates their gift for communication on both the written and spoken levels. She is much more flexible than he as far as other people are concerned, which can be seen by the differences in the finger spacing between the hands and the different angles of the thumbs. Again, both their life and head lines are separated, representing independence and a desire to do things their own way. This could cause a butting of heads.

She would be more apt to win an argument, though, because the length of his Heart line suggests he wants to see the best in his loved ones. A fight just wouldn't be worth the hassle or irritation to him.

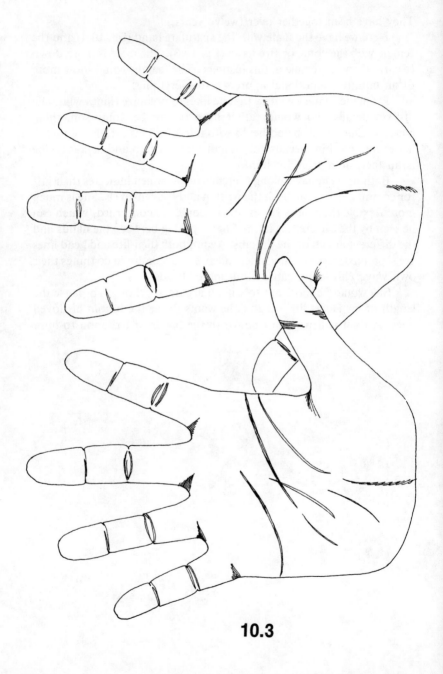

10.3

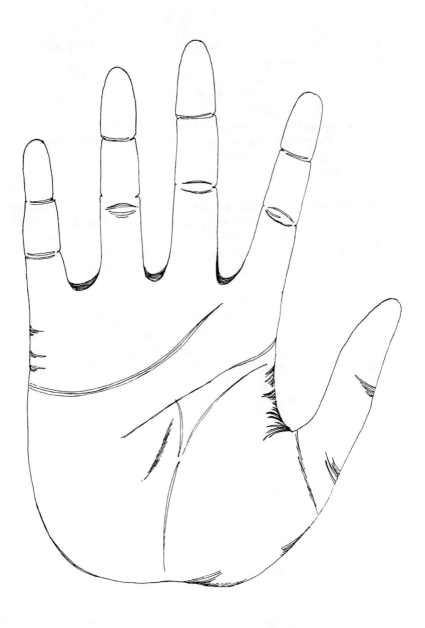

10.4

Couple C

They have been together for three years and got married in June of 1983. Congratulations!

The man shows a strong earth/water hand (fig. 10.5). Look at the square shape of the palm and the short fingers: an indication of either an earth or fire personality.

The squareness is showing a practical and realistic person who wants results and is willing to work hard and plod through to get them. Patience! Patience is what this hand says.

The fingers are at a good arch with the exception of the Mercury finger, which is dipped and is further emphasized by the ring on the right Mercury finger. This is showing a problem with a parental figure — a problem that could have caused feelings of inferiority, especially with sensitive water. The fact that the ring is on the right hand, which is his conscious hand, shows that the problem is out in the open and not buried in the subconscious. This gentleman did have problems with his father.

The woman also has a square hand but with a lot more fire in it (fig. 10.6). She is a steamroller with this earth and fire combination. Her hand speaks of energy. It is alive, like a cat ceaselessly pacing. His hand is much calmer so he will be good for her. Of course, she might sometimes get fed up with his patience, feeling he is not lively enough, but the hands are complementary as a composite.

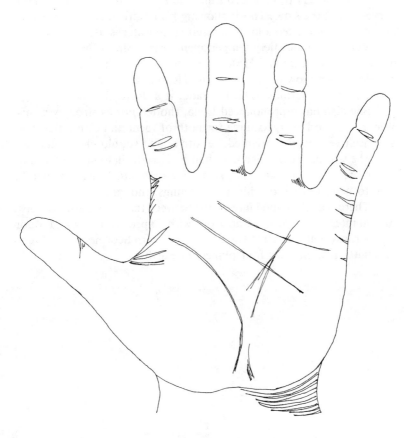

10.5

Her phalanges are well separated though her top phalange on the Mercury finger is pronounced. This shows that she needs sexual intensity and that she would be very inventive in her approach to sex. Good old earth can always take care of those needs. She is a reflexologist and masseuse — an excellent occupation for her sensual nature.

He has a **very** pronounced Luna Mount. (Look at how the mount curves out at the side.) This is showing his intuitive, security-oriented needs. He might keep a lot to himself since water is usually secretive. This could drive her fiery temperament crazy. She is the mover. She has the divided Life and Head lines which say, "I'm independent. I can do it on my own." His Life and Head lines are combined, so he is much more cautious. (He, by trade, is a doctor.)

She also has a pronounced Luna, though not as strongly as his. Water is a good energy source for both of them and shows that they are intuitive, security-oriented, sensitive, and should enjoy animals.

She will be more indecisive than he is with that wavy Head line, and more emotional since her Head line dips into Luna. She will be able to help him get out his inner feelings, though.

There is a lot of good interaction between the two palms. For those of you interested, she is a Capricorn with Capricorn rising and Moon in Taurus. (Hello, Earth!) He is a Scorpio with Scorpio rising, Moon in Sagittarius, and has four planets in Earth.

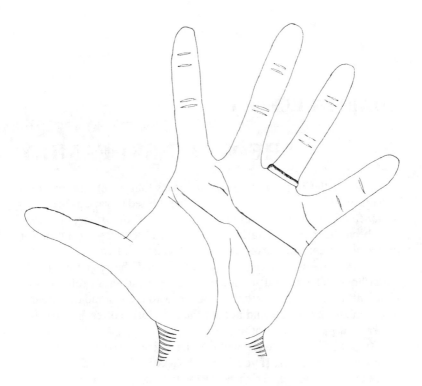

10.6

CHAPTER ELEVEN

THE WALINSKI FAMILY

There is a belief in the field of metaphysics that we choose our own parents and that, usually, we have been connected to various members of our family in previous lives in reversed roles. (For instance, you may have been the mother or father in a previous life and your mother or father at present may have been one of your children.) You see, we all get a chance to experience procreation and the responsibility of parenthood. This affords us the experience of different roles and of different sexual bodies, so that we can grow to understand the integration of male and female and not see them exclusive of each other, but rather as a part of each other.

If you believe in the element of time, these different lives happen in chronological order. If you do not believe in time, then all our different existences and experiences are happening now, at once (possibly an explanation for what we term **schizophrenia** or **split personality**), since these people might be tuning into different existences but are not able to differentiate, and thus cannot function in what is termed a "normal manner").

What follows is a study of the Walinski family, a family I have been connected with over and over in many ways and one that has become a second family to me. It is an interesting study in connections though it is not unique in the experience of family or group *karma*. I want to thank them one and all for allowing me to use them in this book.

There are six children in the family: one boy and five girls. Each child has a 10-year twin. One child was born in 1941, one in 1951; one in 1943, one in 1953; one in 1945, one in 1955 — ten years apart.

Four of the members of this family were born with six digits on their hands, the extra appendage connected to the Mercury finger, which in all cases was surgically removed.

In palmistry, some consider that extra digit a favorable aspect, others consider it a curse. No one seems to know for sure. Anne Boleyn, Henry VIII's second wife, had a sixth digit and though her life ended unhappily (she was beheaded for treason), she was a brilliant orator and gave us Elizabeth I of England.

What I will do in this chapter is take you through the prints of these six individuals — all except for one, who felt uncomfortable with having her palms reproduced. I have included both their numerological and astrological charts so that you can see the connection with all three arts/sciences since they all work together. I included both the mother's and father's palm prints and numerology but not their astrological charts because we were not sure of the time of birth.

We do know that the little Mercury finger represents the winged messenger in mythology. It has to do with communication on all levels: written, spoken and sexual. According to Cyrus Abayakoon in his book, *Astro Palmistry*, the first phalange of the Mercury finger represents Scorpio, the second phalange represents Libra and the third phalange represents Virgo. This is interesting in that both Libra and Scorpio deal with relationships and Scorpio rules the sexual organs. Virgo is ruled by, guess who? Yes! Mercury — so communication and intimate relationships are definitely a part of this finger.[10]

When Patricia Walinski and I asked the Ouija board why the family had a predominance of sixes in both their palms and their numbers, we were told that there had been an overindulgence in the appetites in another lifetime and that they had come back specifically to get beyond the sexual/sensual appetites and use the sexual energy, the serpent-fire, in a more spiritual, teaching way. Please note, there was no judgment concerning the indulgence. Everyone experiences different things at different times. The message was that they were to go beyond that and to teach and help others with their energy. This would have to be through communication on some level, whether it is written, spoken, through teaching, lecturing or in the psychic area.

This was interesting in that the number 6 in numerology can show someone who deserted a loved one in another life, someone who did not take responsibility. It is the number of mankind and the reverse of the number of God, the 9. Six is physical. It represents procreation, artistic pursuits, and is usually connected to the voice and music. It

10. Abayakoon, Cyrus D. F. *Astro Palmistry, Signs and Seals of the Hand*. New York: ASI Publishers, Inc., 1975.

shows that the person has come here to learn how to balance the emotional and mental parts of his personality. It represents **responsibility** and the Star of David or prophecy.

The Twins

Carol Ann Walinski — Born 9/23/1941 (Figures 11.1-11.6)
Dianne Eve Walinski — Born 1/5/1951 (Figures 11.7-11.11)

In numerological terms Carol is an 11/2 life path and Dianne Eve is a 22/4 life path. Both women came in with what is called **master numbers**. This means that they are both old souls and it shows that they have come here to teach in some manner.

Both women have a 5 birthday. Dianne was born on the 5th and Carol was born on the 23d, which in numerology is reduced to a 5. So there would be similarities in their actions in the world.

Both women were born with a sixth digit attached to their Mercury fingers. Except for the thumbs, the fingernails are similar — even their spread is similar. Both girls hold their Mercury fingers apart from the rest of their fingers, showing their independence and the predominance of the fingers' attributes. Carol intensifies this by wearing a ring on her little finger which also shows a preoccupation with her sexual, intimate relationships.

Carol's thumb shows that a lot of her energy is repressed, for she has what is termed a "clubbed thumb." She doesn't release her emotions such as anger or resentment. She needs an outlet for her feelings where she can channel her energies in a constructive manner. She could find this outlet through doing some kind of physical work with her hands such as sculpturing, painting or working with jewelry. It is interesting that Carol has started studying acupressure and the art of massage. What a wonderful way for her to use the energy and to help both herself and others.

When we turn the hands over, the difference in the two women becomes apparent. Carol's hand is much more lined and sensitive. It is dry, even in the picture, which suggests that she is extremely sexual. The nervousness is apparent in the many diversified lines. She is like a finely tuned-in radio that can act as a receiver — a medium. The 11/2 life path talks about being a high-strung, nervous, creative and intuitive person who has to be careful that she does not allow others to use her as a doormat; 11/2s can get into this because they are so open.

Astrologically, Carol is a Libra, ruled by Venus, the goddess of love and beauty. Libra deals with one-to-one relationships and with artistic ability. The 11/2 in numerology also deals with relationships,

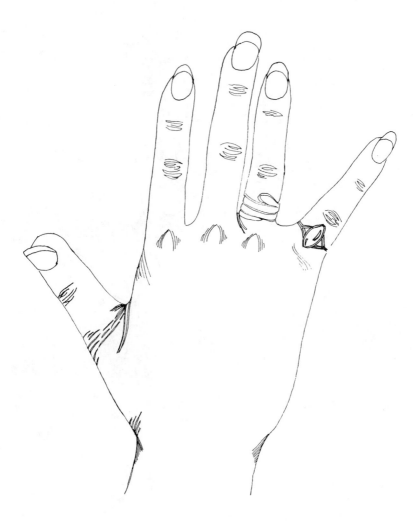

11.1

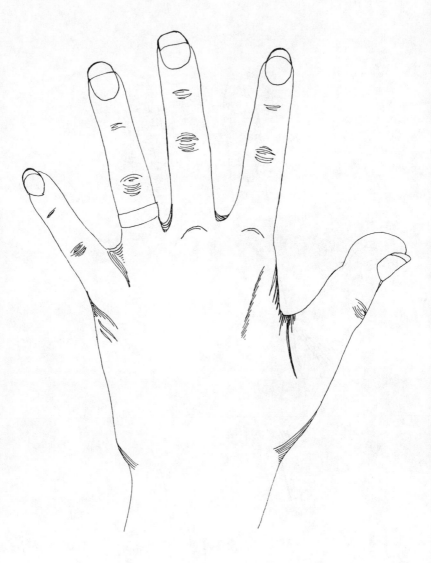

11.2

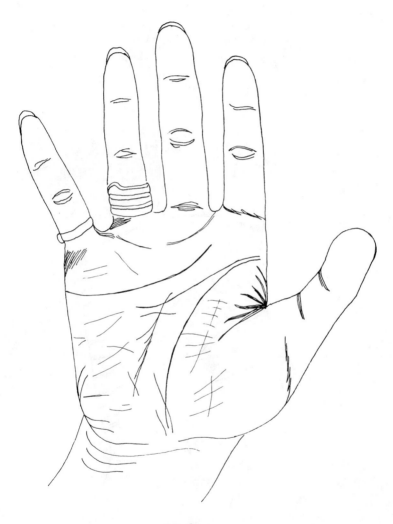

11.3

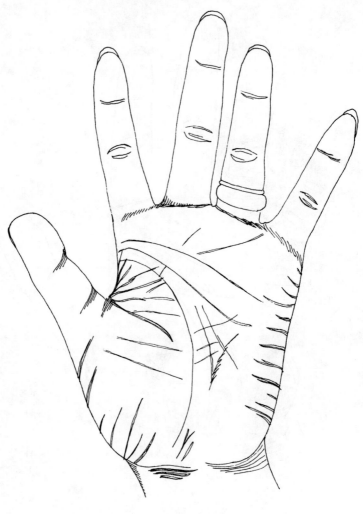

11.4

Carol Ann Walinski

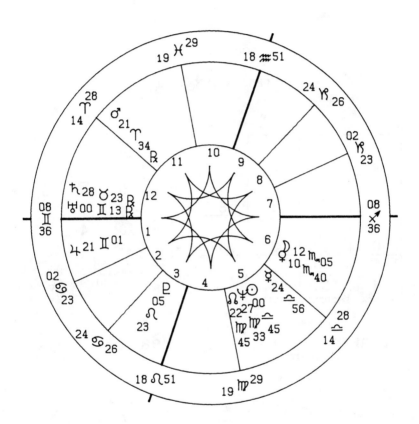

11.5

NAME: **Carol Ann Walinski**
1 6 1   1 9   9
1 9 3   5 5 5   3 5 1 2

BIRTHDATE: **9-23-1941**
5
1

$\frac{7}{15/6}$ **13/4** $\frac{1}{10/1}$ **2** $\frac{19/1}{16/7}$ **8**   LIFE PATH **11/2**   NAME **5**

Power #7

SOUL URGE **9**

PERSONALITY **14/5**

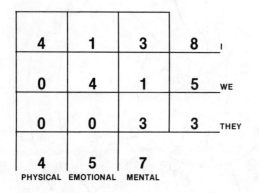

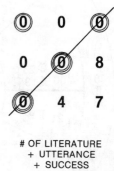

OF LITERATURE
+ UTTERANCE
+ SUCCESS

	4	1	3	8 I
0	4	1	5 WE
0	0	3	3 THEY
4	5	7	
PHYSICAL	EMOTIONAL	MENTAL	

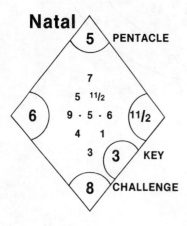

Natal

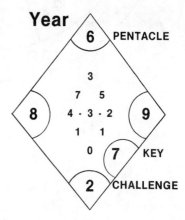

Year

11.6

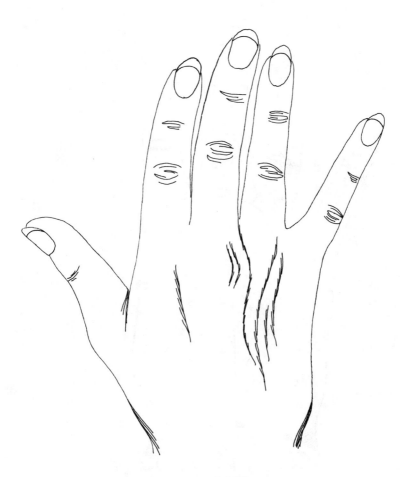

11.7

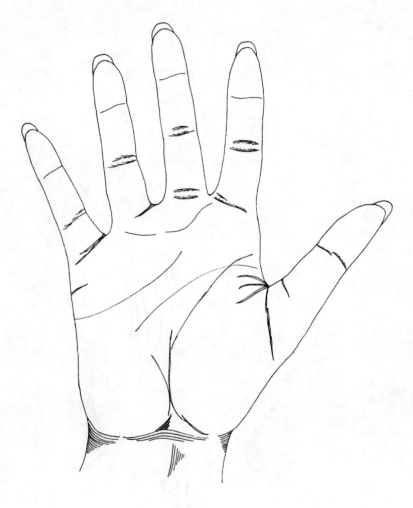

11.8

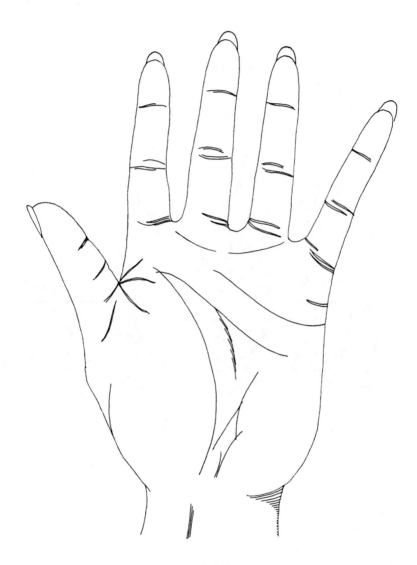

11.9

Dianne Eve Walinski

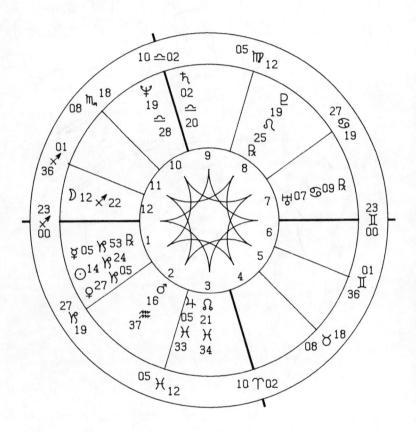

11.10

NAME: **Dianne Eve Walinski**
9 1   5   5   5   1 9   9
4   5 5   4   5   3 5 1 2

BIRTHDATE: **1-5-1951**

| $\frac{14/5}{14/5}$ | **1** | $\frac{10/1}{4}$ | **5** | $\frac{19/1}{16/7}$ | **8** | LIFE PATH | **22/4** | NAME | **6** |

Power #9

SOUL URGE | **8**
PERSONALITY | **16/7**

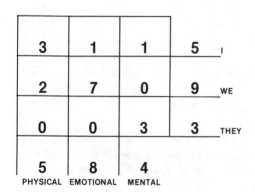

3	1	1	5	I
2	7	0	9	WE
0	0	3	3	THEY
5	8	4		
PHYSICAL	EMOTIONAL	MENTAL		

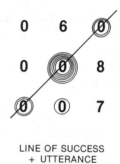

LINE OF SUCCESS
+ UTTERANCE

```
0   6   Ø
0   Ø   8
Ø   Ø   7
```

Natal

```
        9  PENTACLE
        9
      6   3
3   1 · 5 · 7   4
      4   2
      2  6  KEY
        8  CHALLENGE
```

Year

```
        8  PENTACLE
        4
      6   7
2   3 · 3 · 4   1
      0   1
      1  4  KEY
        2  CHALLENGE
```

11.11

beauty and sharing.

It is interesting that on Carol's 7th house cusp she shows that she is looking for a Sagittarius; her 10-year twin, Dianne, has Sagittarius rising. Dianne is looking for a Gemini and Carol has Gemini rising, so they do use each other for projection purposes.

We all use a certain amount of projection in our daily relationships. It means disowning a part of our personality with which we do not feel comfortable and finding another person to express that part of ourselves which we have disowned. By seeing the other person through our own eyes, we are observing a part of our behavior that we cannot deal with yet and that we need to learn about. That is why two people who are very similar often will not get along. They see themselves constantly in the other person and they often don't like what they see.

Carol and Dianne in some ways are acting as mirrors for each other. Notice how much clearer Dianne's hand is — much more the earth type, like her Capricorn Sun and her packed 1st house in Capricorn and her 22/4 life path. One woman is living the high-strung, nervous, artistic and psychic life. (Look at the packed Leo house with the Libra and Virgo combination in Carol's chart showing the artistic craftsman. Carol is a draftsperson.) Dianne is living the more practical, realistic and earthy side.

Both women are psychic (with the master numbers). Both have long, little fingers: Dianne's appears longer because Carol's is low set, showing her need to work on relationships, especially with mom and dad; Dianne's is actually about 1/16" longer.

Dianne would have an easier time channeling her energies because of the clearness of her lines. Carol needs to work with meditation, yoga or hypnosis in order for her to channel her energies in a specific direction. But Carol could easily get into automatic writing or mediumship because she is very receptive.

Note the Girdle of Venus in both hands, showing the artistic, intuitive and literary ability in both women. The psychic area is again stressed.

John Anthony Walinski — Born 3/24/1945 (Figures 11.12-11.16)
Patricia Lynn Walinski — Born 6/7/1955 (Figures 11.17-11.22)

Here we have some interesting interchanges. Patricia was born in the sixth month and her life path number is a 33/6, another master number. John's birth date, in numerology, adds up to a 6 so she and John will

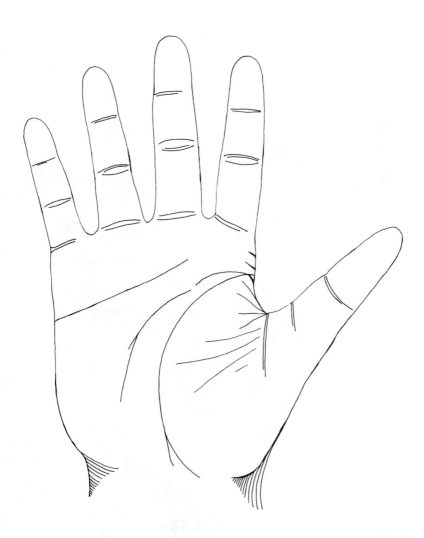

11.12

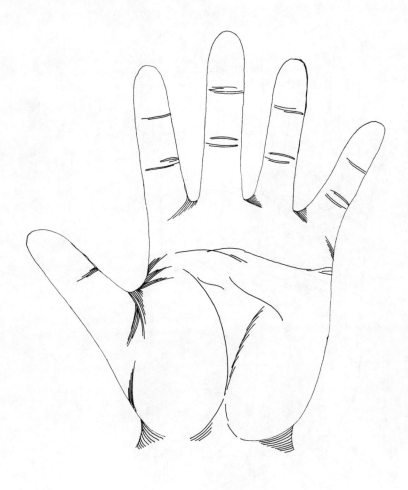

11.13

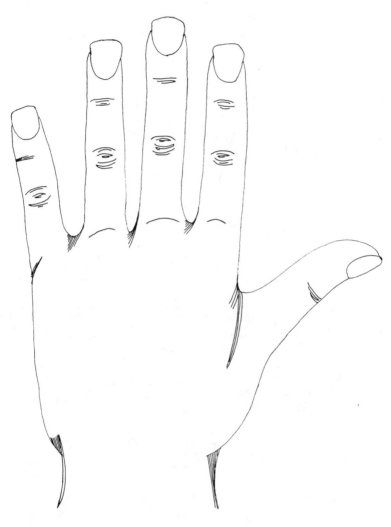

11.14

John Anthony Walinski

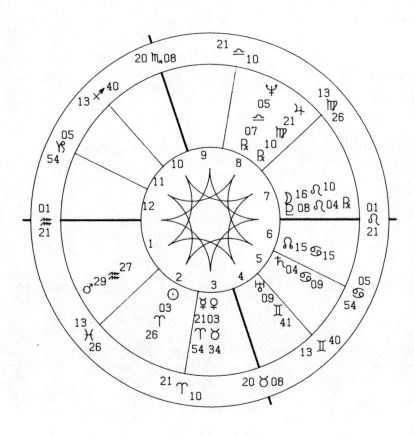

11.15

NAME: **John Anthony Walinski**   BIRTHDATE: **3-24-1945**

Above "John": 6 1
Below "John": 1 8 5

Above "Anthony": 6 7
Below "Anthony": 5 2 8 5

Above "Walinski": 1 9 9
Below "Walinski": 5 3 5 1 2

$\frac{6}{14/5}$ **11/2** $\frac{14/5}{20/2}$ **7** $\frac{19/1}{16/7}$ **8**   LIFE PATH **1**   NAME **8**

Power #9

SOUL URGE **12/3**

PERSONALITY **14/5**

4	2	1	7 ₁
0	5	2	7 WE
1	2	2	5 THEY
5	9	5	
PHYSICAL	EMOTIONAL	MENTAL	

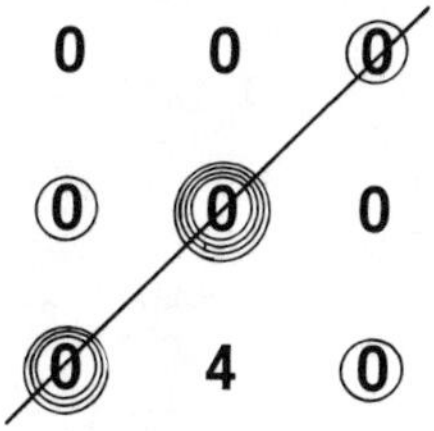

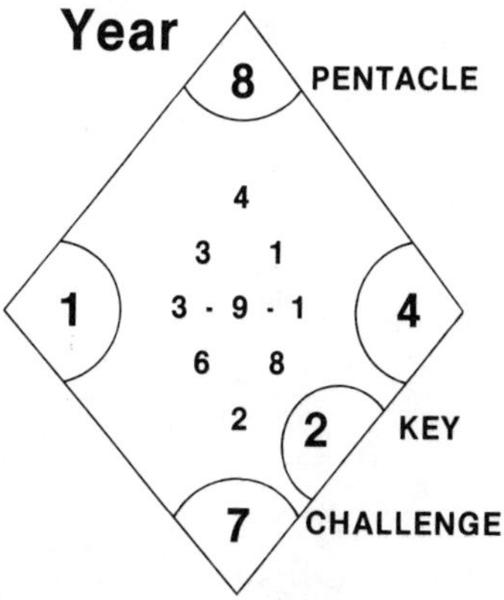

```
  0     0     0

 0     0     0

 0     4     0
```

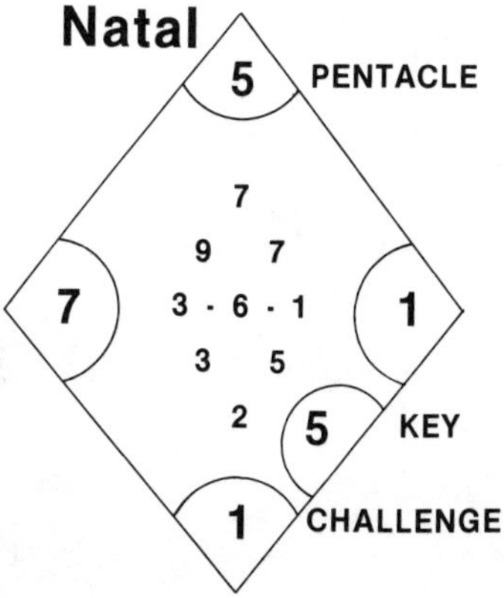

Natal

5 PENTACLE

7

9 7

3 · 6 · 1   1

3 5

2

5 KEY

7

1 CHALLENGE

Year

8 PENTACLE

4

3 1

3 · 9 · 1   4

6 8

2

2 KEY

1

7 CHALLENGE

11.16

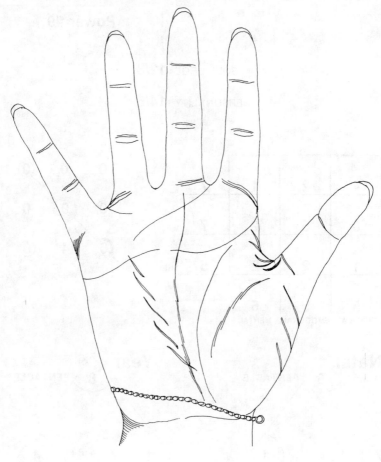

11.17

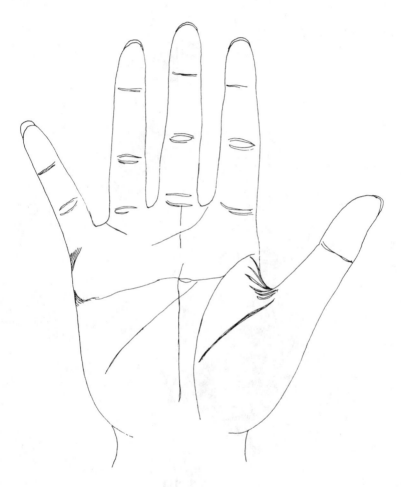

11.18

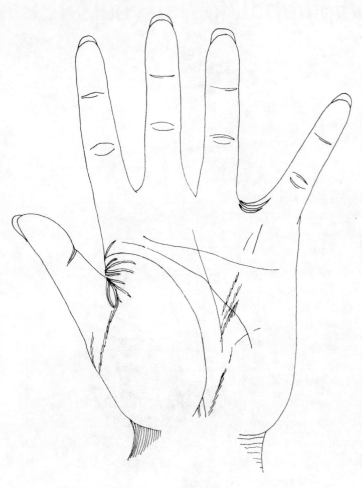

11.19

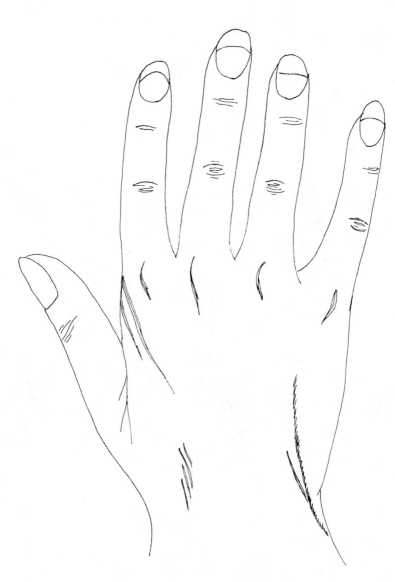

11.20

Patricia Lynn Walinski

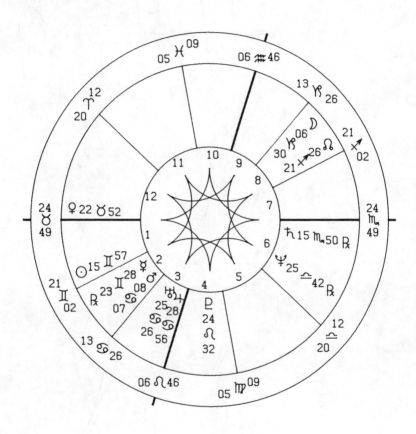

11.21

NAME: **Patricia Lynn Walinski**

BIRTHDATE: **6-7-1955**

$\frac{20/2}{21/3}$ **5** $\frac{7}{13/4}$ **11/2** $\frac{19/1}{16/7}$ **8**   LIFE PATH **33/6**   NAME **6**

Power #3

SOUL URGE **1**

PERSONALITY **5**

6

4	2	3	9	I
0	4	0	4	WE
2	0	5	7	THEY
6	6	8		

PHYSICAL EMOTIONAL MENTAL

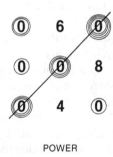

POWER

Natal

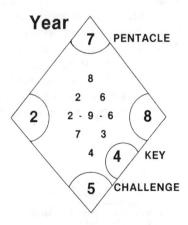

11.22

work in the world in similar ways.

Again, both people were born with six digits and John had six toes. And again, the Mercury finger is long — extremely so in Patricia's case since it looks so straight and pointed, as though it is ready to duel. This points to her sarcastic, cynical tongue.

John is an Aries. Patricia is a Gemini. John and Patricia have strong, physical hands. Both have Lower Mars developed in both hands, showing their ability for the physical world and movement. Again, John and Patricia are psychic. Tricia makes more use of her psychic ability. She does automatic handwriting, is a numerologist, and uses the Ouija board. John lets his little girl Michelle be the psychic for him. He tends to fight his psychic ability more. But look at his Scorpio house showing the psychic power. It is also interesting that Scorpio plays so heavily in this family. John has two planets and four asteroids in the Scorpio house. Carol and Kay both have their Moon in Scorpio. Kay (whom we have not done yet) has Scorpio rising. Patricia has Scorpio on her 7th house angle. Her Moon and her North Node are in her Scorpio house with Pluto, the natural ruler of Scorpio, in Cancer, a sign of psychic ability.

Scorpio in astrology rules the 8th house and represents death and resurrection, as well as partnerships. Note that the family name Walinski adds up to the number 8.

It is interesting that in olden days the 6th and the 8th houses in astrology were under one sign and that Scorpio was ruled by Mars. Maybe that is a clue to the 6 and 8/Scorpio connection with this family.![11]

You will note that John was born in the third month, March, and Tricia was born in the sixth month, June — $3 + 3 = 6$ or $3 \times 2 = 6$.

Patricia has a modified simian line which shows that there is a conflict or tension aspect between the head and the heart. There could be difficulty balancing these two areas.

In John's left hand we have a distinct drop from the Heart line to the Head line, showing that he is allowing his head to rule his heart.

Now we come to the two women in the family who were **not** born with a sixth digit but still play with the 6 and the 8.

---

11. Hone, Margaret E. *The Modern Text Book of Astrology*, London: L. N. Fowler & Co., LTD, 1951.

Joan Marie Walinski — Born 5/24/1943 (Figures 11.23-11.24)
Kay Frances Walinski — Born 10/10/1953 (Figures 11.25-11.28)

Numerologically, right off the bat, we can see that Joan was born in the fifth month and Kay in the tenth month — $5 + 5 = 10$ or $2 \times 5 = 10$.

Joan's cornerstone is the letter J, a 1 number; Kay's cornerstone is the letter K, a 2 number — again, a doubling concept.

Joan will not give me the xeroxed copies of her hand because she does not feel comfortable doing so. We will have to look at her numerological chart and her astrological chart.

Joan has a 6 birth date and has 6 in her family, or "we" column — and in her physical and mental columns as well.

In Kay's chart we see that she has 6 in the physical, emotional and mental columns and that her superpentacle is the number 6. She has Venus, Mars and Ceres in Virgo in the 10th house of occupations, showing an area of work which is of service to others. The same principles of Virgo apply to the numerical attributes of the number 6.

Joan has her North Node and her Pluto, the natural ruler of Scorpio, in her Virgo house. She has Neptune in Virgo in her 7th house of partnerships. Both Kay and Joan have their Moons in the 12th house, again showing a *karmic* connection.

Kay's Uranus is on top of Joan's Jupiter. Joan's Pluto is conjunct Kay's Juno and her North Node is conjunct Kay's Pallas — both partnership aspects. Like Carol and Dianne, there is a lot of projection going on here.

Kay's handprint (figs. 11.25 & 11.26) shows her Mercury finger to be long, emphasizing her unusually artistic, business and communication skills. She is also psychic. Her 11/2 life path, her Moon and Mercury in Scorpio in the Pisces house, her Uranus in Cancer in her Scorpio house, and her Neptune in Libra in her Aquarian house verify this. Both Kay and Joan back away from the psychic area. It does not seem to be as strong a focus for them as it is for the rest of the family.

When Joan was born, 1943, the universal year was an 8. Joan has an 8 personality number, which shows that others see her as powerful, in control and usually sarcastic.

Joan Marie Walinski

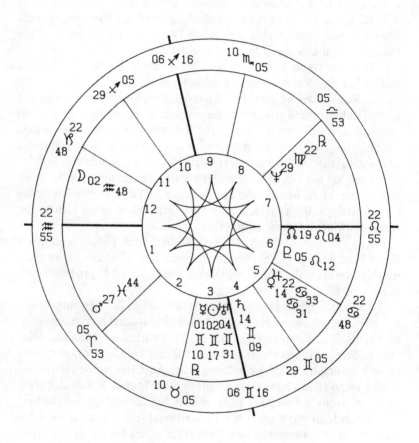

11.23

NAME: **Joan Marie Walinski**

BIRTHDATE: **5-24-1943**

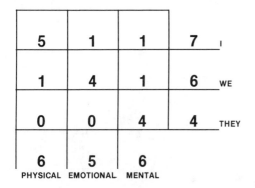

LIFE PATH **1**   NAME **13/4**

Power #5

SOUL URGE **14/5**

PERSONALITY **17/8**

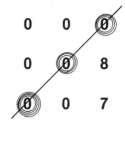

5	1	1	7 ₁
1	4	1	6 WE
0	0	4	4 THEY
6	5	6	
PHYSICAL	EMOTIONAL	MENTAL	

Natal

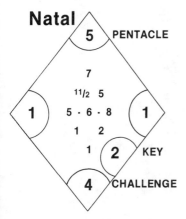

Year

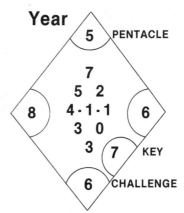

11.24

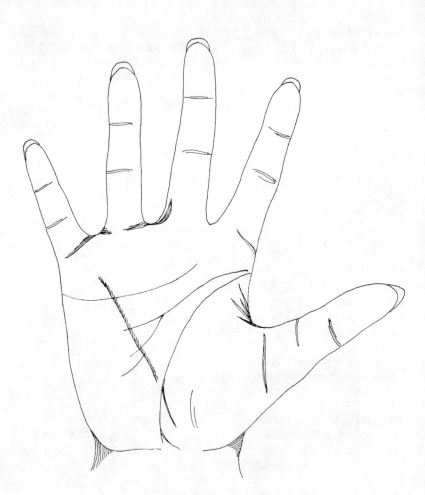

11.25

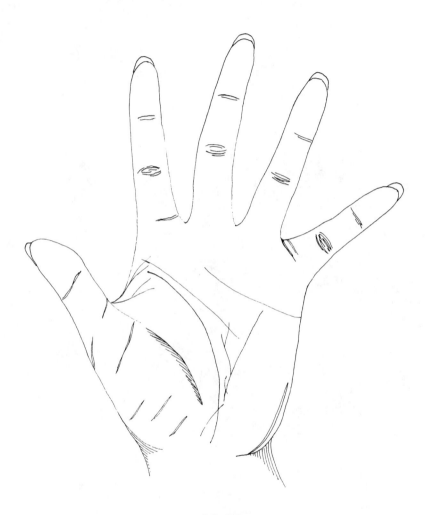

11.26

Kay Frances Walinski

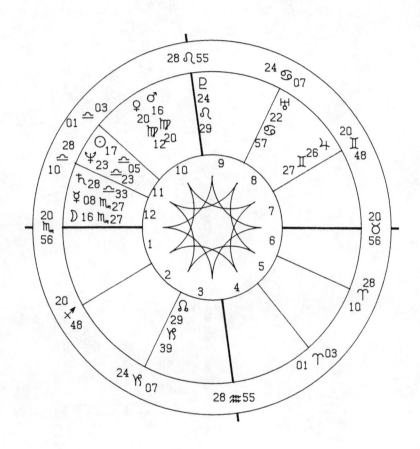

11.27

NAME: **Kay Frances Walinski**

BIRTHDATE: **10-10-1953**

$\frac{1}{9}$ **10/1** $\frac{6}{24/6}$ **12/3** $\frac{19/1}{16/7}$ **8**   LIFE PATH **11/2**   NAME **12/3**

Power #5

SOUL URGE **8**

PERSONALITY **4**

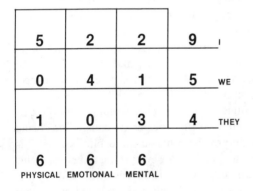

5	2	2	9 ı
0	4	1	5 WE
1	0	3	4 THEY
6	6	6	

PHYSICAL   EMOTIONAL   MENTAL

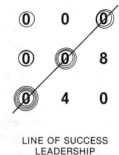

LINE OF SUCCESS
LEADERSHIP
LITERATURE

Natal

6 PENTACLE

3
2 1
1 · 1 · 9   11/2
0 8
8   3 KEY

7 CHALLENGE

Year

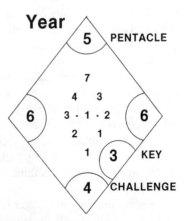

5 PENTACLE

7
4 3
3 · 1 · 2   6
2 1
1   3 KEY

4 CHALLENGE

11.28

Boy Walinski — Born 9/17/1911 (Figures 11.29-11.31)
(known as Daniel Walinski)
Cacelia Kusteliski — Born 5/12/1916 (Figures 11.32-11.34)

We can't really look at the six children and not pay attention to the mother and father. So, except for the astrology charts, here we go.

We are using the name Boy Walinski because in numerology you use the name the child was born with even if that name is Baby Boy or Baby Girl. There is a reason for all things. The name finally given brings a certain vibration with it but it does not alter the personality inherited at birth.

If you look at Daniel's print, you see that the little finger is extremely long. He was **not** born with a sixth digit, nor was Cecelia. The length of Daniel's Mercury finger shows the communication ability and, if spiritually oriented, the ability for teaching, lecturing and mediumship. Daniel is also an 11/2 birth date, just like his daughters Carol and Kay. (Please note the amount of master numbers in these charts.)

Daniel is a 7 soul urge and personality number — a strong statement stressing his mind, his intuitive abilities, his analytical abilities, and showing that he came here to work with the mental side and introspection. (That can be a pretty good trick with six children.)

The length of Daniel's fingers shows a very mental person. One of the things that can happen with a 7 is that the person can get into being overcritical of both himself and of the others around him because 7 is the number of the perfectionist. The 7 wants everything to be just right, and if it isn't, the person can get very upset. Sevens don't usually like a lot of noise, which again is a little difficult with six children. If you look at Daniel's Venus Mount, you will see many lines crossing the mount. This shows that he can get into overanalyzing and into guilt. He can allow others to interfere with him.

Cecelia also has an 11/2, as you can see in her first name and in her "1" column. Here again we have a very nervous and sensitive person. She, in contrast to Daniel, has 3s all over her inclusion table, which deals with communication on both the written and spoken levels as well as with creativity. (She decided to create by having six children.) Everyone in this family, grandchildren included, are into crafts of some sort.

If you look at Cecelia's palm prints, she, like her daughter Carol has the many fine lines running through her hand, correlating with her 11/2 life path.

Again, the Mercury finger is not just long, but it is bent in toward the hand. This not only accentuates the qualities of the finger, but also

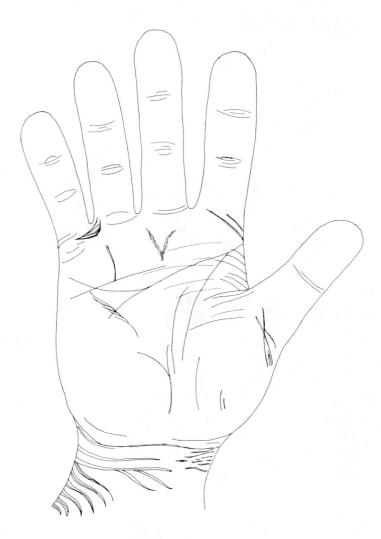

11.29

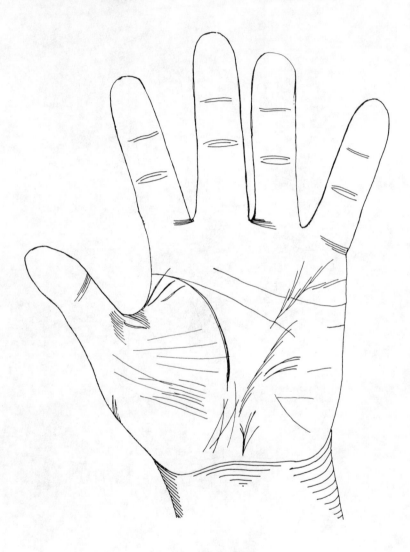

11.30

NAME: **Boy Walinski**
$\overset{6}{B}o\overset{1\ 9}{y}\ \overset{9}{W}alinski$
2 7 5 3 5 1 2

| 11 |

BIRTHDATE: **9-17-1911**
8
6

$\frac{6}{9}$ | 15/6 | $\frac{19/1}{16/7}$ | 8 |

LIFE PATH | 11/2 | NAME | 5 |

Power #7

SOUL URGE | 7 |

PERSONALITY | 7 |

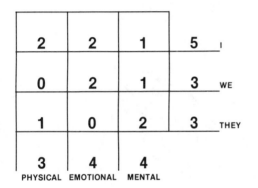

2	2	1	5	I
0	2	1	3	WE
1	0	2	3	THEY
3	4	4		
PHYSICAL	EMOTIONAL	MENTAL		

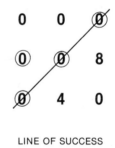

LINE OF SUCCESS

0 0 0̸

0̸ 0̸ 8

0̸ 4 0

Natal

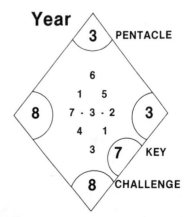

2 PENTACLE

1
8 11/2
9 · 8 · 3   11/2
1   5
4   1 KEY

1 CHALLENGE

Year

3 PENTACLE

6
1 5
8   7 · 3 · 2   3
4   1
3   7 KEY

8 CHALLENGE

5

11.31

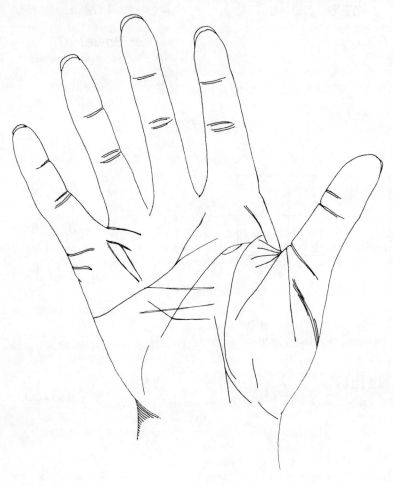

11.32

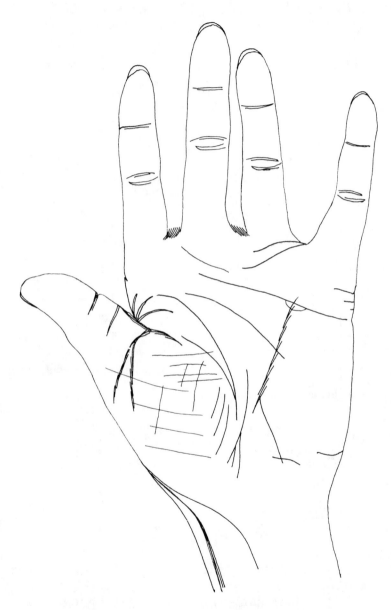

11.33

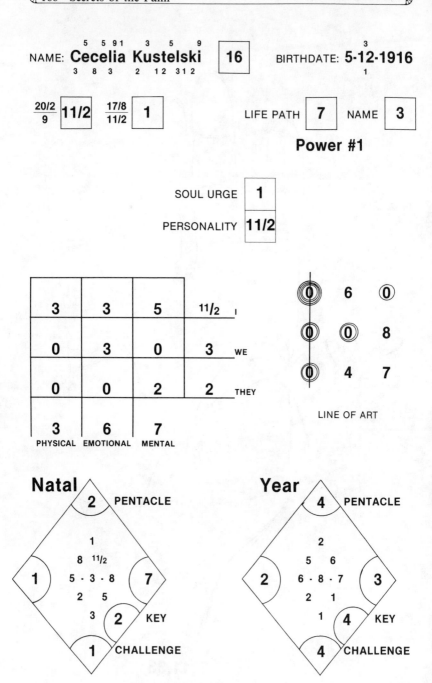

NAME: **Cecelia Kustelski**   16   BIRTHDATE: **5-12-1916**

5 5 9 1   3   5   9
3 8 3   2   12   31 2

3
1

$\frac{20/2}{9}$ **11/2** $\frac{17/8}{11/2}$ 1   LIFE PATH   7   NAME   3

Power #1

SOUL URGE   1

PERSONALITY   **11/2**

3	3	5	**11/2** I
0	3	0	3 WE
0	0	2	2 THEY
3	6	7	
PHYSICAL	EMOTIONAL	MENTAL	

0   6   0
0   0   8
0   4   7

LINE OF ART

Natal

2   PENTACLE

1
8   11/2
1   5 · 3 · 8   7
2   5
3   2   KEY

1   CHALLENGE

Year

4   PENTACLE

2
5   6
2   6 · 8 · 7   3
2   1
1   4   KEY

4   CHALLENGE

11.34

shows that she might not have made use of her abilities since the bending takes away a certain amount of the qualities represented in her finger.

The conclusion is that a sixth digit added to the hand does indicate the owner has an ability in the communicative skills: lecturing, sales, teaching and writing.

It does, however, ask of its owner that there be a balance between the physical/materialistic plane and the spiritual/artistic plane. How the owner decides to use the abilities is up to himself.

I hope that this chapter is as interesting to you as it has been to me in looking at group *karma* and the connections between parents and children. I have included a breakdown of all the members of the family and hope you will continue the study.

WALINSKI FAMILY

Boy Walinski	Soul Urge:	7	Date of Birth: 9/17/1911
	Personality:	7	Sun: Virgo
	Name:	5	Palm: Air/Water
	Life Path:	11/2	
	Power Number:	7	
Cecelia Kusteliski	Soul Urge:	1	Date of Birth: 5/12/1916
	Personality:	2	Sun: Taurus
	Name:	3	Palm: Fire/Earth
	Life Path:	7	
	Power Number:	1	
Carol Ann Walinski	Soul Urge:	9	Date of Birth: 9/23/1941
	Personality:	5	Sun: Cusp of Libra/Virgo
	Name:	5	Palm: Predominantly Air
	Life Path:	11/2	
	Power Number:	7	
Dianne Eve Walinski	Soul Urge:	7	Date of Birth: 1/5/1951
	Personality:	7	Sun: Capricorn
	Name:	5	Palm: Earth/Air
	Life Path:	22/4	
	Power Number:	9	
John Anthony Walinski	Soul Urge:	3	Date of Birth: 3/24/1945
	Personality:	5	Sun: Aries
	Name:	8	Palm: Fire/Earth
	Life Path:	1	
	Power Number:	9	
Patricia Lynn Walinski	Soul Urge:	1	Date of Birth: 6/7/1955
	Personality:	5	Sun: Gemini
	Name:	6	Palm: Air/Water
	Life Path:	33/6	
	Power Number:	3	
Joan Marie Walinski	Soul Urge:	5	Date of Birth: 5/24/1943
	Personality:	8	Sun: Gemini
	Name:	4	Palm: Unavailable
	Life Path:	1	
	Power Number:	5	
Kay Frances Walinski	Soul Urge:	8	Date of Birth: 10/10/1953
	Personality:	4	Sun: Libra
	Name:	3	Palm: Water/Air
	Life Path:	11/2	
	Power Number:	5	

CHAPTER TWELVE

EPILOGUE

In order to become the knower of **self**, thou hast first of **self** to be the knower.

— Book of the Golden Precepts
(Tibetan Buddhist Scripture)

You have journeyed with me through the valley of the hand. The information presented is not conclusive of truth but then I don't feel that truth can always be found or understood in our concrete world.

There is much too much evidence that exists in regards to the miracle of the human body that we don't fully comprehend as yet. We have only touched upon a small section of that unique miracle through the study of the palm.

Remember that you are constant energy traveling through the dimension of time in a body frame that is a part of your reality. The palm is a section of that experience, an experience to help you know "**self**."

Love,

Darlene

SELECTED BIBLIOGRAPHY

Abayakoon, Cyrus D. F. *Astro Palmistry, Signs and Seals of the Hand*. New York: ASI Publishers, Inc., 1975.

Aria, Gopi. *Morningland, Palmistry for the New Age*. Long Beach: Morningland Publication, 1977.

Bashir, Mir. *How to Read Hands*. Westport, Conn.; Associated Booksellers, 1956.

Your Past, Your Present and Your Future Through the Art of Hand Analysis. New York: Doubleday & Co., Inc., 1974.

Benham, William G. *The Law of Scientific Hand Reading*. New York, London: G. P. Putnam's Sons, 1900.

Broekman, Marcel. *The Complete Encyclopedia of Practical Palmistry*. Englewood Cliffs; Prentice-Hall, Inc., 1972.

Cavendish, Richard. *Man, Myth, and Magic*, vol. 16. New York: Marshall Cavendish Corp., 1977.

Cummins, Harold, and Midlo, Charles. *Finger Prints, Palms and Soles*. New York: Dover Publications, 1961.

Dangaard, Colin. "Ten Thousand Hands." *Psychic* (December 1974): 40-43.

Encyclopedia of Occultism and Parapsychology. vol. 2. Detroit: Gale Research Co., 1978.

Gettings, Fred. *The Book of the Hand*. London: Hamlyn, Ltd., 1965.

— -. *Palmistry Made Easy*. North Hollywood: Melvin Powers, 1975.

Hipskind, Judith. *Palmistry, the Whole View*. Saint Paul: Llewellyn Publication, 1977.

Hone, Margaret E. *The Modern Textbook of Astrology* London, England: L.N. Fowler & Co., Ltd., 1951

Jeffrey, Barbara. "Your Health Is in Your Hands." *Family Circle*(June 14, 1978, Vol. 91, Number 7): 96-97, 140-141, 160.

Lawrance, Myrah. *Hand Analysis*. West Nyack: Parker Publishing Co., 1967.

Leadbeater, C. W. *The Chakras*. Wheaton, Ill.: The Theosophical Publishing House, 1929.

Saint, Germain, Comte C. de. *The Practice of Palmistry*. London: Newcastle Books, 1973.

Steinbach, Marten. *Medical Palmistry*. New York: New American Library, 1975.

Walker, Benjamin. *Man, the Beast Within*. New York: Stein and Day Publishers, 1977.

Wilson, Joyce. *The Complete Book of Palmistry*. New York: Bantam Book, 1971.

Wolff, Charlotte. *The Hand in Psychological Diagnosis*. New York, NY: Philosophical Library, 1952.

INDEX

A

alcoholism 45, 49
arch of the fingers 19
arthritis 45

B

beau's lines 13-14

C

cancer 45, 47, 49
children lines 110-113
conscious hand 1
compatability 117-127

D

diabetes 45, 47, 49

F

fate line
   start of, 98-100
   ending of 99-100
   markings on 101-102
   timing 101-102
female disorders 47, 49
fingernails
   conic 3, 4
   filbert 3-5
   long and Narrow 4-5
   medium 4-5
   pointed 3-4
   short 4-5
   spatulate 3-4
   square 3-4
   wide 4-5
   pink-colored 12
   red-colored 12
   pale-colored 12
   blue-colored 12
   scooped 13-14
   watchglass 13-14

fingers
   Jupiter 33-34, 36
   knotty 19-21
   Mercury 34-35, 37-38
   smooth 19-21
   Saturn 33-34, 36-37
   Uranus 34-35, 37
fingerprint patterns
   arch 22-24
   radial loop 23-24
   ulnar loop 23-24
   whorl 24-26

G

girdle of Venus 113-116
glandular disturbances 47-49

H

hair 2
head line
   beginning of 87-89
   ending of 88-89, 91
   markings on 88, 90-91
heart line
   beginning of 92
   course of 93-94
   length of 92, 94
   markings on 93, 95-96
high-strung person 48-49

J

Jupiter Mount
   displacement of 57-59
   markings on 58-59

L

long fingers 17-18
long-narrow palm 18
life line
   beginning of 80-81

life line (cont.)
  ending of 80-82
  arc of 82, 84
  markings on 82-86
  timing 85-86
lower Mars
  displacement of 73
  markings on 75-76
major/minor hand 1
Mee's lines 14-15
Mercury finger 34-35, 37-38
Mercury line
  start of 105-106
  ending of 105-106
  markings on 105
Mercury Mount 64-65
  displacement of 64
  markings on 64-65
Mongoloid 48-49

P
Pluto Mount
  markings on 68-69

S
Saturn finger 33-34, 36-37
Saturn Mount 58, 60-61
  displacement of 60
  markings on 60-61
shape of the palm
  square 40-41, 52
  round 42-43
  philosophical 42, 44, 53
  psychic 42, 46
short fingers 17
short-wide palm 18
Simian line 95-97
skin texture 2
spacing
  between fingers 6-9
  between hands 6-7
Sun line

start of 103-104
  ending of 103
  markings on 103-104
Sun Mount
  markings on 73-74

T
thumb
  angle 30-31
  clubbed 31-32
  flat 31-32
  length of 28-30
  narrow-waisted 31-32
  rhythm knot 31, 33
  sections of 29-30
  stiff 31-32
  supple thumb 31-32
  width of 31-32

U
unconscious hand 1
union lines 107-109
  markings on 108-109
  age on 108
Upper-Mars Mount
  displacement of 66
  markings on 66-67
Uranus finger 34-35, 37
Uranus Mount
  displacement of 62
  markings on 62-63

V
Venus Mount 70-73
  displacement of 71
  markings on 71-73
vertical lines on nails 13-14

W
Walinski family, 128-170

We calculate... You delineate!